Cocaine:
Pharmacology, Addiction, and Therapy

Cocaine: Pharmacology, Addiction, and Therapy

Guest Editors
Mark S. Gold, MD
Marc Galanter, MD
Editor
Barry Stimmel, MD

The Haworth Press
New York • London

Cocaine: Pharmacology, Addiction, and Therapy has also been published as *Advances in Alcohol and Substance Abuse*, Volume 6, Number 2, Winter 1986.

The Haworth Press, Inc., 12 West 32 Street, New York, NY 10001
EUROSPAN/Haworth, 3 Henrietta Street, London WC2E 8LU England

Library of Congress Cataloging-in-Publication Data

Cocaine—pharmacology, addiction, and therapy.

Includes bibliographies.
1. Cocaine habit.   2. Cocaine—Physiological effect.   3. Methadone maintenance.
4. Cocaine habit—United States.   I. Gold, Mark S.   II. Galanter, Marc.
III. Stimmel, Barry, 1939–   [DNLM: 1. Cocaine.
2. Substance Abuse.   WM 280 C6598]
RC568.C6C63   1987   616.86′4   86-29392
ISBN 0-86656-615-5

Cocaine:
Pharmacology, Addiction,
and Therapy

Advances in Alcohol & Substance Abuse
Volume 6, Number 2

CONTENTS

EDITORIAL

Cocaine: A New Epidemic

The plant, Erythroxylon Coca, has been used by societies for thousands of years. In the Inca Empire, the Emperor controlled its use, with the right to chew the coca leaf valued above silver or gold.[1] Although in 1844, the alkaloid cocaine, comprising 0.5 to 11% of the plant's dry weight, was actually isolated from coca leaves, the best known and most comprehensive report of the effects of cocaine was by Freud in 1884.[2] This scientific discourse found cocaine to be effective in the treatment of numerous disorders, including morphine addiction and alcoholism. Unfortunately, Freud did not immediately realize the adverse mood-altering effects and dependency associated with its use. His recognition of cocaine's potential for abuse was of such an intensity that he subsequently attempted to eliminate all mention of its therapeutic effects from his autobiography.

Knowledge of the stimulant properties of cocaine continued to spread throughout society, resulting in its addition to various over-the-counter preparations and elixirs in the early 1900s. One of the most popular preparations was Coca-Cola, which contained cocaine until 1906.[3] Cocaine use was subsequently tightly controlled by the Harrison Narcotic Act of 1914, with its use for other than its local anesthetic properties prohibited.

The illicit use of cocaine as a stimulant and euphoric, although ever present, until recently was perceived as a relatively minor problem. Cocaine use was restricted to those in the "hard-core" drug culture, frequently associated with heroin use, or was seen as the drug of the glamorous and of those in the Arts. It was viewed rather benignly by the public, with prevalent medical opinion being somewhat tolerant. [Cocaine was considered neither physically addictive nor capable of causing serious medical complications, aside from those associated with illicit injection. Unfortunately, all of this has proven incorrect.] [1]

The dangers of cocaine use in laboratory animals have been well demonstrated by Johanson et al. [4] Monkeys allowed to self-administer cocaine will choose it over food and water until starvation. Most chilling, however, has been the recent publication by Bozarth and Wise, who demonstrated self-administration of cocaine to be three times as lethal as heroin, with 90% of animals with free access to cocaine dying within three months as compared to 30% of those having access to heroin. [5] Cocaine related mortality in humans, however, has never been adequately documented and, therefore, of little concern.

In the late 1970s, for reasons which remain less than clear, but undoubtedly related to the marked drop in the price of cocaine, its prevalence began to increase and has now reached epidemic levels, affecting over 22 million people in all strata of society. Although initial widespread use occurred through snorting, in an effort to achieve an even greater high freebasing became popular. With this technique a more dangerous form of cocaine was produced by combining the adulterated cocaine with either a baking soda or evaporating the mixture over a flame. Most recently, a new form of cocaine is appearing known in the street as Crack. [Crack is "purified" cocaine which can be immediately smoked or freebased.] With increasing use, have appeared more frequent reports of physical dependence and cocaine related morbidity and mortality. [Between 1982 and 1983, as reported by the National Institute on Drug Abuse, there has been a 91% increase in cocaine-related deaths. [6]]

This issue of *Advances* reviews the current state of knowledge of cocaine use, its toxicity and the potential therapeutic modalities that may be used to address this problem. Consistent with the philosophy of *Advances*, the first paper by Dackis et al., reviews the neurochemistry and pharmacology of central stimulant abuse, focusing on the specific effects of cocaine.[7] It is only through a knowledge of the basic sciences that one can adequately formulate a comprehensive treatment approach.

The next series of papers address recent experiences concerning the epidemiology of cocaine use from several different data bases. Gottheil presents this problem from the view of the epidemiologist.[8] Washton and Gold focus on the National Cocaine Hotline, a toll-free nationwide line providing assistance to individual cocaine users and/or their families.[9] A third data base, that of the National Institute of Drug Abuse, as presented by Adams et al., describes reports from the DAWN Network comprising emergency room and hospital admission and mortality data, linking the use of cocaine with marijuana and that of other drugs.[10] Newcomb and Bentler review their experiences with cocaine use in young adults.[11] The combined use of heroin and cocaine in heroin addicts is reassessed by Hanbury et al.,[12] and Hunt et al.[13] Not surprisingly, cocaine use among people in methadone maintenance is considerable and, not infrequently, use by injection rather than snorting persists.

The diagnosis of cocaine use in an individual with an established pattern of heavy use is not difficult. Loss of attention, increased activity and weight loss are frequently observed. Identification of the intermittent user is more difficult. As discussed by Lehrer and Gold, diagnosis by body fluid analysis is more complex than previously realized, and reliance solely on this technique may well result in a number of cocaine users going undetected.[14]

Once a diagnosis is made, treatment is necessary. This may involve inpatient or outpatient detoxification, as reviewed by Dackis et al.,[7] structured group therapy, as described by Washton,[15] or the existence of an office practice network, as presented by Galanter.[16] Nationally, a network of Cocaine Anonymous (CA) chapters is beginning to emerge, attracting a growing number of persons who appear to benefit from this mutual aid. The CA program parallels that of Alcoholics Anonymous and, when employed after intensive social intervention in an inpatient setting, may serve as an adjunct to ambulatory therapy or even as a definitive treatment.

Additional application of therapeutic social networks, particularly those employing families, are likely to gain support as they already have in the field of alcoholism treatment.[17] Intensive, inpatient rehabilitation may also be necessary to avoid protracted periods of heavy use and to break the powerful conditioning effects of the drug. All of these approaches merit continued investigation through well-designed studies.

In the field of pharmacologic therapy, a wide variety of agents already in use for other disorders are now showing signs of promise in treating cocaine dependency. Based on our current knowledge of neurochemistry, tricyclic antidepressants have been suggested as effective in relieving the cocaine craving and preventing relapse.[18,19] Controlled studies, however, are needed to determine the effectiveness of this approach. More recently, the use of bromocriptine, a dopamine agonist, has been shown in selected patients to relieve cocaine craving, possibly by interfering with cocaine's role in central nervous system stimulation.[20] Lithium carbonate, previously investigated in the treatment of alcoholism, also shows some promise for facilitating abstinence in certain cocaine-dependent individuals.[19] Unfortunately, published studies of these drugs' effectiveness are neither large nor well designed. Much more efforts are needed.

While medical treatments for detoxification are improving and certain drugs may be helpful in eliminating cocaine-seeking behavior, long-term abstinence will require motivation, association with a drug-free family, a strong peer recovery network, close monitoring of program attendance and even urine testing.

Equally important, although not addressed in this issue, is the need for an effective preventive approach. Unfortunately, little published information exists concerning effective prevention. Until the public can be adequately educated about the adverse effects of cocaine, its spread through all strata of society will continue. The need for public support of basic and clinical research in all aspects of cocaine use remains great. The use of cocaine is far from being contained and its adverse, long-term effects yet to be fully realized.

Mark S. Gold, M.D.
Marc Galanter, M.D.
Barry Stimmel, M.D.

REFERENCES

1. Blejer HP. Coca leaves and cocaine addiction—Some historical notes. Canad Med Assoc J. 1965;93:701.

2. Byck R. Cocaine papers by Sigmund Freud. New York: Stonehill Publishing Company, 1978.

3. Brecher EM. Licit and illicit drugs: the Consumers Union Report. Boston: Little Brown & Co., 1972.

4. Johanson CE, Balster RL, Bonese K. Self-administration of psychomotor stimulant drugs. The effects of unlimited access. Pharmacol Biochem Behav. 1976; 4:45–51.

5. Bozarth MA, Wise RA. Toxicity associated with long-term intravenous heroin and cocaine self-administration in the rat. JAMA. 1985; 254:81–3.

6. Pollin W. The danger of cocaine. JAMA. 1985; 254:98.

7. Dackis CA, Gold MS, Pottash ALC. Central stimulant abuse: neurochemistry and pharmacotherapy. Advances in Alcohol & Substance Abuse. 1986–87; 6(2):

8. Gottheil E. Cocaine abuse and dependence: the scope of the problem. Advances in Alcohol & Substance Abuse. 1986–87; 6(2):

9. Washton AM, Gold MS. Recent trends in cocaine abuse: a view from the National Hotline, "800-COCAINE." Advances in Alcohol & Substance Abuse. 1986–87; 6(2):

10. Adams EH, Gfroerer JC, Rouse BA, Kozel NJ. Trends in prevalence and consequences of cocaine use. Advances in Alcohol & Substance Abuse. 1986–87; 6(2):

11. Newcomb MD, Bentler PM. Cocaine use among young adults. Advances in Alcohol & Substance Abuse. 1986–87; 6(2):

12. Hanbury R. Sturiano V, Cohen M, Stimmel B, Aquillaume C. Cocaine use in persons on methadone maintenance. Advances in Alcohol & Substance Abuse. 1986–87; 6(2):

13. Hunt D, Spunt B, Lipton D, Goldsmith D, Strug D. The costly bonus: cocaine related crime among methadone treatment clients. Advances in Alcohol & Substance Abuse. 1986–87; 6(2):

14. Lehrer M, Gold MS. Laboratory diagnosis of cocaine: intoxication and withdrawal. Advances in Alcohol & Substance Abuse. 1986–87; 6(2):

15. Washton AM. Structured outpatient treatment of cocaine abuse. Advances in Alcohol & Substance Abuse. 1986–87; 6(2):

16. Galanter M. Social network therapy for cocaine dependence. Advances in Alcohol & Substance Abuse. 1986–87; 6(2):

17. Ehrlich P. McGeehan M. Cocaine recovery—support groups and the language of recovery. J Psychoactive Drugs. 1985; 17:11–18.

18. Tennant FS. Rawson RA. Cocaine and amphetamine dependence treated with desipramine. In: Harris LS, ed. Problems of drug dependence. NIDA Research Monograph #43, Rockville, Maryland, 1982.

19. Gawin FH, Kleber HD. Cocaine abuse treatment. Arch Gen Psychiat. 1984; 41:903–9.

20. Dackis CA, Gold MS. Bromocriptine as treatment of cocaine abuse. (Letter), Lancet. 1985; 2:1151–2.

Central Stimulant Abuse:
Neurochemistry and Pharmacotherapy

Charles A. Dackis, MD
Mark S. Gold, MD
A. L. C. Pottash, MD

ABSTRACT. This paper reviews certain clinical and neurochemical aspects of cocaine abuse. Once entrenched patterns of addiction have developed, cocaine addicts suffer progressive financial, medical, psychiatric and psychosocial deterioration that results, to some extent, from cocaine-induced neurochemical alterations in the brain. While cocaine produces euphoria through its stimulatory effect on dopamine neurons, several lines of evidence suggest that dopamine depletion occurs after chronic cocaine abuse. The dopamine neurotransmitter system is therefore a natural starting point for understanding the biology of cocaine addiction and selecting suitable adjunctive pharmacological agents. Furthermore, the dopamine depletion hypothesis implies that cocaine is "physically" addictive and provides a biological framework for understanding this disease and refining present therapeutic approaches.

INTRODUCTION

Cocaine is currently the major central stimulant of abuse in the United States, with epidemic levels of addiction becoming evident. Similarly, the abuse of amphetamines exists on a worldwide basis and threatens to resurface in the United States if or when cocaine use wanes. Indeed, there is a substantial demand for central stimulants that undoubtedly stems from their euphorogenic property. The natural history of stimulant abuse includes intoxication and withdrawal states, progressive repercussions of addiction, and psychological features of chronic use. Clinical and neurochemical aspects of central stimulant abuse must be understood before effective

---

Dr. Dackis is Medical Director at Hampton Hospital, P.O. Box 7000, Rancocas, NJ 08073.

Dr. Gold and Dr. Pottash are affiliated with Research Facilities, Fair Oaks Hospital, Summit, NJ 07901.

7

treatments can be formulated. Pharmacological actions of central stimulants on endogenous reward centers produce acute intoxication effects, while protracted neurochemical disruptions in the brain appear to be associated with withdrawal and craving states. Compelling evidence now exists that cocaine is physically addictive, based on measurable neurochemical alterations and clinical observations. This paper will outline biological and phenomenological aspects of stimulant abuse, based on our experience interviewing and treating cocaine addicts, and on research into biological alterations and treatments of this condition.

THE NATURE OF THE DISEASE

As with all forms of addictive illness, the natural history of cocaine abuse involves a progressive process that begins with recreational use, and evolves gradually to compulsive addictive patterns that encompass and dominate all aspects of the addict's life. Severe cocaine addicts become obsessed with cocaine euphoria, and are subject to frequent and almost irresistible craving. Cocaine euphoria and craving are the predominant reinforcers of severe addiction, and must be addressed by any viable treatment. While addicts often furnish a number of reasons and excuses why they use drugs, it is generally for the attainment of pleasure and alleviation of craving. These reinforcers have both psychological and biological bases, which will be further discussed later.

In order to understand and delineate the nature of cocaine abuse, we have collected data supplied by a large number of cocaine addicts calling our national hotline (800-COCAINE). This service has been in place for approximately two years, and we have received over one million calls from cocaine users and their relatives. Epidemiological and phenomenological information is collected from cocaine users who call our hotline seeking treatment referrals or information about cocaine. While methodological problems clearly exist with this form of data collection, the anonymous feature of phone interviews might also allow for more accurate responses than would be obtained under more controlled situations.

According to our 800-COCAINE surveys, point prevalence and lifetime prevalence have been relatively stable over the past 2 years. However, cocaine use by adolescents is on the rise, as evidenced by a 6% frequency of cocaine use by high school seniors in our 1984 survey. There now appears to be a core group of 4–5 million regular cocaine users. Since cocaine use often progresses to severe and entrenched addiction, a stable and younger group of users would be expected to yield increasing numbers of seriously addicted users over time. Consistent with this notion is the finding by the Drug Abuse Warning Network (DAWN) that cocaine emergency room visits are increasing at an alarming rate (from 10 per 100,000 visits in 1983 to 75 per 100,000 at present). Similarly, there has been a tremendous increase in hospitalizations and outpatient treatments for cocaine abuse. These epidemiological data support the concept of "progression", or the automatic worsening of addiction over time, that is well appreciated in alcoholism and opiate dependence. However, with cocaine abuse, a much shorter time appears sufficient for the development of entrenched patterns of addiction and lack of control over drug use.

In order to evaluate present trends in cocaine abuse, we recently conducted two separate surveys in the New York area. The first was done in May of 1983 and the second in May of 1984. The most recent survey (Table 1) shows an increase in the number of female users, and a shift toward younger age groups. A higher percentage of lower income users was also evident. Less than 50% are now earning over $25,000 per year, with more students, blue collar and clerical workers, and housewives than were found in the 1983 sample. These data indicate that, although cocaine is exceedingly expensive, cost factors do not discourage use by individuals who are becoming increasingly dependent on the drug.

The frequency of use and route of administration are important factors that characterize cocaine use. Table 2 includes callers who

TABLE 1
Demographics of Cocaine Addicts
(N = 200)

	1983	1984
Males	76%	58%
Females	24%	42%
White	81%	84%
Black/Hispanic	19%	16%
Income > $25,000	52%	40%
Age (mean yrs.)	31	28.5
Education (mean yrs.)	13.2	14.1

TABLE 2
Severity of Cocaine Abuse
(N = 200)

	1983	1984
Duration of use (mean yrs.)	4.6	3.5
Intranasal users	58%	60%
Freebase users	16%	27%
Grams per week (mean)	5.5	6.2
Cost per week (mean)	$450	$430
Other drug/alcohol abuse	66%	75%

used cocaine for periods ranging from several months to 15 years. Most were intranasal users, although nearly all intravenous and freebase (smoking cocaine crystal) users began as intranasal users. During the one year between surveys, the freebase route of administration has increased and the intravenous method has decreased. The incidence of intranasal use has remained virtually unchanged. Since freebase and intravenous routes are essentially interchangeable with regard to brain cocaine delivery, a shifting from intravenous use does not represent a decrease in addiction severity. The weekly amount of cocaine used by our callers has increased, as have concomitant abuses of other drugs and alcohol. This represents a progression of polysubstance abuse, or "chemical dependency", in these individuals. Other drugs are often used to counter adverse effects of cocaine, such as restlessness, irritability, depression, paranoia and overstimulation. It should be noted that the combined use of cocaine and other drugs or alcohol can be extremely dangerous. One example of this is seen in users who become rapidly stuperous from previously ingested depressants when the acute effects of cocaine wear off. This situation can occur when users are driving, or engaged in other critical activities.

We addressed the issue of addiction with anonymous surveys. Table 3 reveals that the majority of cocaine users calling our hotline believe that they are addicted to cocaine. They clearly describe an inability to limit their use or refuse the drug when it is present. Often these users fear pay increases because their purchases of cocaine might increase. Most of the callers are unable to abstain from cocaine for one month, feel distressed without it, and prefer cocaine to almost everything else in their lives. We found that 76% of users have increased their dose or shifted to freebase use in order to maintain an adequate "high" from the drug. These individuals clearly feel addicted and complain of withdrawal symptoms when cocaine use is abruptly stopped. They also make life choices that are characteristic of drug addicts. Often these patients continue to use cocaine in spite of significant medical consequences, psychotic reactions, and family or job repercussions. The issue of whether they are addicted is seldom in question by the time they call the hotline. We found that 80% believe cocaine is physically addictive, and 75% believe they are physically addicted. Therefore, user reports run contrary to the popular concept that cocaine is not addicting.

Table 4 evaluates the psychosocial consequences of cocaine abuse by illustrating the deterioration of conduct in serious cocaine users. The development of antisocial behaviors and shifting of values are characteristic of addictive illness. The increase in cocaine related auto accidents is of particular interest, and analogous to the alcoholic's loss of prudent judgment. Stealing, drug sales, and other illegal acts likewise illustrate how cocaine use becomes the addict's first priority. The addict's willingness to tolerate psychosocial deterioration and hazards of cocaine use further indicates the addictive power of this drug.

Most textbooks of pharmacology state that the abrupt discontinua-

---

TABLE 3

Elements of Addiction; Self-reports
(N = 200)

	1983	1984
Feel addicted	63%	74%
Loss of control	74%	85%
Cannot refuse if offered	85%	85%
Unable to stop for 1 month	70%	76%
Feel distressed without it	52%	61%
Prefer cocaine to food, family, friends and recreation	70%	73%
Describe withdrawal symptoms	66%	75%

TABLE 4
Adverse Psychosocial Effects
(N = 200)

	1983	1984
Dealing cocaine to support habit	43%	47%
Stealing from work	20%	28%
Stealing from family or friends	28%	42%
Arrests for dealing or possession	17%	14%
Auto accidents on cocaine	9%	39%
Loss of job due to cocaine	16%	15%
Loss of spouse due to cocaine	30%	33%
In debt due to cocaine	46%	57%

tion of chronic cocaine use is not associated with signs and symptoms of physical dependence. However, severe users report feeling unable to stop[1] and describe a group of subtle "crashing" symptoms.[2] We have found that these symptoms include anergia, hypersomnia, hyperphagia, amotivation, irritability, paranoia, decreased libido, and nausea. Interestingly, cocaine craving frequently wanes during the "crash", but returns several days later. "Crashing" symptoms presumably depend on dose and duration factors, in much the same way that opiate withdrawal varies with the severity of opiate use. Since the actual quantity of cocaine use is usually difficult to assess, the amount of cocaine exposure required to precipitate withdrawal symptoms is somewhat unclear. In cases of significant withdrawal, pharmacological treatment may be indicated to re-establish neurochemical balance. We have hypothesized a dopamine (DA) depletion model to explain cocaine withdrawal and more protracted craving. This hypothesis and possible pharmacological approaches to cocaine abuse will be described in the next sections.

PLEASURE CENTERS IN THE BRAIN

Cocaine's rewarding power can be seen in the willingness of animals to self-administer the drug in preference to sex, food and water,[3] thus overriding basic survival drives. In fact, animals will self-administer cocaine to the point of severe toxicity and death.[4] Cocaine addicts likewise prefer cocaine euphoria over other pleasurable activities, and will continue their addiction in the face of hazardous medical, psychiatric and psychosocial repercussions. Cocaine addiction cannot be adequately understood without appreciating the reinforcing power of the cocaine intoxication state. Extensive research in several fields, particularly involving intracranial electrical stimulation,[5] has indicated the presence of specific neural substrates of reward.[6] These brain regions may be related to the mechanisms of natural drive reduction or incentive reward. Since cocaine activates the same regions that support electrical self-stimulation,[6] its use may be analogous to the satisfaction of a primary drive. Thus, the craving for cocaine that develops with cocaine addiction might be viewed as an "acquired primary drive". Interestingly, while natural drive reduction reward leads to satiation of the active drive, cocaine use seems to induce or potentiate the drive to consume cocaine. One explanation of this curious phenomenon is that cocaine may rapidly deplete dopamine, which is intimately involved in the neurochemistry of reinforcement.[6] The dopamine depletion hypothesis, and its bearing on cocaine craving, will be developed later.

In his classic studies in the 1950's, Olds found that certain discrete brain regions, which he named "pleasure centers",[5] would support electrical self-stimulation in animals. Since that time, much research has been directed toward delineating the neurochemistry and neuroanatomy of endogenous reward systems in the brain. It is now apparent that central dopamine systems are intimately involved in these pathways.[6] In particular, descending reward fibers from the lateral hypothalamus project via the medial forebrain bundle to the ventral tegmentum, where they appear to synapse with major dopamine cell groups.[6,7] In fact, the interruption of dopamine neurotransmission blocks electrical self-stimulation of the lateral hypothalamus.[8] The ventral tegmentum in turn projects to several other striatal, limbic and cortical dopamine areas. Specific lesions of these dopamine-containing nuclei will block the direct self-administration of cocaine into these areas.[9,10,11] Similarly, selective dopamine receptor antagonists reduce or eliminate cocaine self-administration by animals,[12] and central stimulant euphoria in humans.[13,14] These and other findings[6,15] indicate that the activation of dopamine circuits appears to mediate cocaine reward in animals, and cocaine euphoria in humans.

DOPAMINE DEPLETION HYPOTHESIS

Central stimulants acutely activate dopamine circuits by blocking the synaptic reuptake of dopamine.[16] However, based on a number of neurochemical findings (See Table 5), we have hypothesized that chronic cocaine abuse depletes brain dopamine.[15,17] Increased dopamine receptor binding[18] and reduced brain dopamine levels after chronic exposure to cocaine are consistent with decreased dopamine availability at the postsynaptic receptor.[19] Cocaine administration also leads to increased tyrosine hydroxylase activity,[20,21] indicating compensatory dopamine synthesis. We evaluated dopamine function in a number of chronic cocaine addicts by measuring serum prolactin levels, which were increased in both male[22] and female[23] cocaine addicts during their first week of cocaine abstinence. Since prolactin secretion is under inhibitory regulation by tuberoinfundibular dopamine neurons,[24] these elevated prolactin levels are consistent with dopamine depletion. Clinical and preclinical data therefore suggest that dopamine depletion results from chronic cocaine administration.

It has been previously hypothesized that reuptake blockade leads to dopamine depletion by exposing released dopamine to synaptic

TABLE 5

Effects of cocaine on dopamine neurons

Acute dopamine activation secondary to dopamine reuptake blockade

Increase in synaptic dopamine acutely

Increased dopamine neurotransmission acutely

Increased levels of synaptic dopamine metabolites

Chronic effects consistent with dopamine depletion

Tyrosine hydroxylase activation (increased dopamine synthesis)

Increased postsynaptic dopamine receptor binding

Reduction in brain dopamine

Inhibition of dopamine vesicle binding

metabolism.[15,25] Since dopamine is normally bound in secretory vesicles and reutilized after its reuptake, chronic cocaine use would prevent this "recycling" of dopamine by interfering with its reuptake (see Figure 1). Instead, dopamine appears to be synaptically metabolized, as evidenced by increased 3-methoxytyramine levels with cocaine administration.[26]

FIGURE 1

Dopamine Shunt

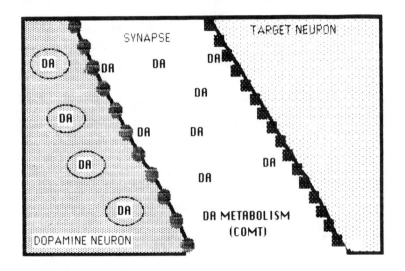

● Dopamine reuptake site: Cocaine blocks these sites

■ Dopamine receptor (post-synaptic): Bromocriptine stimulates these receptors

Cocaine blocks dopamine reuptake from the synapse, exposing released dopamine to synaptic metabolism by catechol-O-methyl transferase. Reuptake blockade leads to a "dopamine shunt" by interfering with the normal recycling of released dopamine, leading to dopamine depletion.

Dopamine Depletion and Craving

Severe and chronic cocaine abusers often "crash" after abruptly ceasing their cocaine use. "Crashing" symptoms include anergia, amotivation, decreased concentration, decreased libido, depression, hypersomnia, irritability, headaches and hyperphagia. While these symptoms may last only 3 to 5 days, cocaine craving often persists for long periods of time, and will resurface with environmental stimuli. Craving has significant clinical importance because it often preceeds recidivism in recovering addicts. We have hypothesized that cocaine craving might result from dopamine depletion.[15,25] This biological basis for cocaine craving would be analogous to that with cocaine euphoria, which depends on the activation of dopamine brain circuits.[6,27] A vicious cycle of dopamine potentiation followed by dopamine depletion may be established in cocaine abuse, with a progressive exhaustion of endogenous reward systems in the brain.

PHARMACOTHERAPY IN COCAINE ADDICTION

Although cocaine abuse, like all forms of addiction, is a biological illness, there are no widely prescribed biological treatments at present. Current treatments rely on drug rehabilitation utilizing proven methods borrowed from alcoholic's anonymous, and other self-help group approaches. However, cocaine craving and withdrawal might respond to pharmacotherapy. Pharmacological agents might also serve to block the cocaine high. While the reduction of craving and blockade of euphoria are not sufficient treatments in and by themselves, these adjuncts might complement the process of recovery.

Preliminary pilot studies have reported anti-craving and euphoria-blocking efficacy with the largely noradrenergic agent, desipramine.[28] While the efficacy of desipramine in cocaine craving remains unclear, it should be recalled that dopamine and not noradrenaline is the critical catecholamine involved in cocaine reward.[6] The dopamine neuronal system might therefore be a more logical substrate for the pharmacotherapy of cocaine-induced subjective states, since cocaine euphoria and perhaps cocaine craving are based predominantly on disruptions of dopamine neuronal function. If cocaine craving stems from dopamine inhibition or depletion, symptomatic relief of craving might be attained pharmacologically with dopaminergic agonists. Cocaine addicts describe frequent, almost irresistible urges to use cocaine. The compelling nature of this craving can be appreciated by the fact that animals will preferentially self-administer central stimulants over all "natural" reinforcers, including food, water and mating opportunities.[29] Actually, the "natural" drives of appetite and thirst are probably mediated to some extent by dopamine circuits, since pimozide blocks food and water reinforcement.[6,30] Craving in the cocaine addict might therefore be comparable to or exceed the intensity of severe thirst, hunger, and sexual desire. If cocaine craving results from disruptions of endogenous reward systems in the brain, such as dopamine depletion, it might be viewed as an "acquired primary drive." While drug rehabilitation furnishes a number of effective techniques for the reduction of craving, an effective pharmacological treatment for cocaine craving would be a useful adjunct in the management of these patients.

In order to test the hypothesis that cocaine craving results from dopamine depletion, we administered bromocriptine to a number of cocaine addicts. Anticraving action with this dopamine receptor agonist was found in acute[31] and maintenance[15] trials. Our initial single-blind study[31] utilized extremely low doses of bromocriptine (0.625 mg. orally) for the acute treatment of cocaine craving in recently abstinent addicts, with dramatic anti-craving action over a period of several hours. In all cases, patients were able to distinguish bromocriptine from placebo with regard to craving reduction.[31]

The choice of bromocriptine for the treatment of cocaine craving was based on the dopamine depletion hypothesis.[15,25] Interestingly, this dopamine agonist normalizes increased postsynaptic receptor density[18] and hyperprolactinemia,[22,23] which are two neurochemical alterations associated with chronic cocaine abuse. The apparent efficacy of low dose bromocriptine might be explained by the dopamine receptor supersensitivity produced by cocaine exposure.[18] We are presently assessing single dose challenge and maintenance bromocriptine treatment with a double-blind research design in recently abstinent, hospitalized cocaine addicts. Maintenance treatment for cocaine craving initially involves the oral administration of low dose bromocriptine (0.625 mg. t.i.d.) with a gradual increase in dose, depending on the resolution of craving. The challenge dose we have selected to treat already present craving is 1.25 mg. orally. If the results of our single-blind study are replicated, low-dose bromocriptine might provide a suitable means of treating early cocaine craving, and perhaps later craving precipitated by environmental cues or life stressors. Further research should clarify the efficacy of bromocriptine and address specific treatment regimens. Bromocriptine has not induced euphoria in any of our patients. Similarly, animal studies show that bromocriptine is minimally self-administered, and can not substitute for cocaine as a discriminative stimulus.[32] The apparent lack of significant euphorogenic activity may be related to bromocriptine's postsynaptic site of action (see Figure 1). Cocaine, on the other hand, acts presynaptically by blocking reuptake sites, with an indirect effect on postsynaptic receptors. Cocaine therefore acts on both the presynaptic and postsynaptic neurons that define the dopamine synapse, whereas bromocriptine stimulates only the postsynaptic neuron. This distinction might somehow explain the vast difference between these two dopamine agents with regard to euphoria and reward.

Dopamine Antagonist Treatment

Dopamine receptor antagonists have been shown to block amphetamine-induced euphoria in humans.[13,14] These agents might therefore have a similar blocking action with cocaine euphoria. Cocaine-induced euphoria is a positive reinforcer of continued use, alternating with the negative reinforcer of cocaine craving. A drug capable of blocking cocaine euphoria might therefore have a clinical role in the treatment of cocaine addicts, similar to the adjunctive role served by naltrexone in the treatment of opiate addiction.[33] Future research might therefore be directed toward trials of neuroleptics as a means of blocking cocaine euphoria.

Even if neuroleptics prove to be effective as euphoria-blocking agents, their use in cocaine abusers must be judiciously weighed against a number of possible complications. Obviously, tardive dyskinesia is a possible danger with neuroleptic treatment that must be considered by the physician and patient before neuroleptic treatment is entertained. Neuroleptics might also exacerbate craving during early abstinence, based on our preliminary studies.[15] The ability of neuroleptics to produce craving in cocaine patients should therefore be suspected. We have also reported that cocaine addicts can be extremely sensitive to extrapyramidal side effects of neuroleptics during early abstinence.[15] This vulnerability may result from dopamine depletion secondary to chronic cocaine abuse. If proven effective, neuroleptic treatment might be considered in high risk addicts who do not experience increased craving, or significant side effects from these medications. Further research is necessary, however, before the efficacy and safety of neuroleptic treatment for the blockade of cocaine euphoria can be fully evaluated.

Pharmacotherapy of the Cocaine "Crash"

No current pharmacological treatment is widely prescribed for cocaine withdrawal. This is probably because "crashing" symptoms are relatively brief in duration, and do not occur with all cocaine users. However, with outpatients, cocaine withdrawal might serve to perpetuate the addiction by rendering the addict dysfunctional and in need of cocaine just to attend work or other responsibilities. Cocaine withdrawal might involve dopamine and noradrenaline depletion. If this is the case, precursor loading with L-tyrosine could reverse some of the "crashing" symptoms described by addicts. Along these lines, the efficacy of L-tyrosine in cocaine withdrawal has been previously reported in one open study.[34] "Crashing" symptoms might also result from a relatively hypothyroid state.[35] To the extent that "crashing" symptoms result from dopamine depletion, bromocriptine treatment may also be effective. Further research into the duration of cocaine withdrawal, its frequency in recently abstinent addicts, and the effectiveness of proposed agents is indicated before actual regimens can be proposed.

CONCLUSIONS

This paper has reviewed certain clinical and neurochemical aspects of cocaine abuse. Our 800-COCAINE data indicate that cocaine addicts feel addicted, and are unable to control their intake of the drug once entrenched patterns of addiction have developed. These patients continue to use cocaine even while they suffer financial, medical, psychiatric and psychosocial deterioration. The neurochemical basis of cocaine action on the brain further suggests that it is an addictive agent. Cocaine exerts its euphorogenic action on the brain's endogenous systems of reward. Since dopamine is intimately involved in endogenous reward circuits, and cocaine has profound effects on dopamine neurons,[36] this neurotransmitter system is a natural starting point for understanding the biology of cocaine addiction, and selecting suitable pharmacological agents to be used in this condition. The dopamine depletion hypothesis is consistent with cocaine being a "physically" addictive substance of abuse. If this hypothesis holds, agents such as bromocriptine or other dopamine agonists may have an important role in reversing "physical" disruptions of cocaine abuse. Ultimately, phenomena such as drug euphoria, drug withdrawal, craving, and the progression of addiction might be better understood, and more effectively treated. However, psychological treatments involving an ongoing process of recovery through self-help groups and emotional growth remain the most powerful approaches to cocaine addiction. While pharmacological and biological treatments might serve as useful adjuncts in treatment, the addict must ultimately make essential choices and sacrifices in order to avoid the everpresent risk of readdiction.

REFERENCES

1. Washton AM, Gold MS, Pottash ALC: Intranasal cocaine addiction. *Lancet 2*: 1374, 1983.

2. Resnick RB, Schuyten-Resnick E: Clinical aspects of cocaine: Assessment of cocaine abuse behavior in man. In Mulé SJ (ed.), *Cocaine: Chemical, biological, clinical, social and treatment aspects*. Ohio, CRC Press, 1976, p. 217.

3. Pickens R, Harris WC: Self-administration of d-amphetamine by rats. *Psychopharmacologia* 12: 158–163, 1968.

4. Deneau GA, Yanagita T, Seevers MH: Self-administration of psychoactive substances by the monkey. *Psychopharmacologia* 16: 30–48, 1969.

5. Olds J: Pleasure centers in the brain. *Sci Am* 195: 105–116, 1956.

6. Wise RA: Neural mechanisms of the reinforcing action of cocaine. *NIDA Research Monograph*, 1985.

7. Corbett D, Wise RA: Intracranial self-stimulation in relation to the ascending dopaminergic systems of the midbrain: A movable electrode mapping study. *Brain Res* 185: 1–15, 1980.

8. Fouriezos G, Wise RA: Pimozide-induced extinction of intracranial self-stimulation: Response patterns rule out motor or performance deficits. *Brain Res* 103: 377–380, 1976.

9. Roberts DCS, Koob GF, Klonoff P, Fibiger HC: Extinction and recovery of cocaine self-administration following 6-OHDA lesions of the nucleus accumbens. *Pharmacol Biochem Behav* 12:781–787, 1980.

10. Monaco AP, Hernandez L, Hoebel BG: Nucleus accumbens: site of amphetamine self-injection: comparison with the lateral ventricle. In: *The Neurobiology of the Nucleus Accumbens*, edited by Chronister RB, DeFrance JF, New Brunswick, Maine, Haer Institute, 1980, pp. 338–342.

11. Goeders NE, Smith JE: Cortical dopaminergic involvement in cocaine reinforcement. *Science* 221: 773–775, 1983.

12. Yokel RA, Wise RA: Increased lever pressing for amphetamine after pimozide in rats: Implications for a dopamine theory of reward. *Science* 187: 547–549, 1975.

13. Gunne LM, Anggard E, Jonsson LE: Clinical trials with amphetamine blocking drugs. *Psychiatr Neurol Neurochir* 75:225–226, 1972.
14. Angrist B, Lee HK, Gershon S: The antagonism of amphetamine-induced symptomatology by a neuroleptic. *Am J Psychiatry* 131: 817, 1974.
15. Dackis CA, Gold MS, Davies RK, and Sweeney DR: Bromocriptine treatment for cocaine abuse: The dopamine depletion hypothesis. *Int J Psychiatry Med* 15: 125–135, 1985.
16. Ross SB, Renyi AL: Uptake of some tritiated sympathomimetic amines by mouse brain cortex in vitro. *Acta Pharmacol Toxicol* 24: 297–309, 1966.
17. Gold MS, Dackis CA: New insights and treatments: Opiate withdrawal and cocaine addiction. *Clin Ther* 7: 6–21, 1984.
18. Taylor D, Ho BT, Fagen JD: Increased dopamine receptor binding in rat brain by repeated cocaine injections. *Commun Psychopharmacol* 3: 137–142, 1979.
19. Raff M: Self-regulation of membrane receptors. *Nature* 259: 265–266, 1976.
20. Taylor D, Ho BT: Neurochemical effects of cocaine following acute and repeated injection. *J Neurosci Res* 3: 95–101, 1977.
21. Patrick RL, Barchas JD: Potentiation by cocaine of the stimulus-induced increase in dopamine synthesis in rat brain striatal synaptosomes. *Neuropharmacology* 16:327, 1977.
22. Dackis CA, Estroff TW, Gold MS: Hyperprolactinemia in cocaine abuse. *Am Psych Assoc Abstr*, NR 181, 1985.
23. Dackis CA, Gold MS, Estroff TW, Sweeney Dr: Hyperprolactinemia in cocaine abuse. *Soc Neurosci Abst* 10:1099, 1984.
24. MacLeod RM: Regulation of prolactin secretion. In: *Frontiers in Neuroendocrinology*, edited by Martini L, Ganong WF, New York, Raven Press, 1976, 169–194.
25. Dackis CA, Gold MS: New concepts in cocaine addiction: The dopamine hypothesis. *Neurosci Biobev Rev* 9: 469–477, 1985.
26. DiGiulio AM, Groppetti A, Cattabeni F, et al.: Significance of dopamine metabolites in the evaluation of drugs acting on dopamine neurons. *Eur J Pharmacol* 16: 171, 1971.
27. Wise RA: Brain dopamine and reward. In: *Progress in Psychopharmacology*. Edited by Cooper SJ, New York, Academic Press, 1981, pp. 165–196.
28. Gawin FH, Kleber HD: Cocaine abuse treatment; open pilot trial with desipramine and lithium carbonate. *Arch Gen Psychiatry* 41: 903–909, 1984.
29. Pickens R, Harris WC: Self-administration of d-amphetamine by rats. *Psychopharmacologia* 12:158–163, 1968.
30. Wise RA, Spindler J, DeWit H, Gerber GJ: Neuroleptic-induced "anhedonia" in rats: Pimozide blocks the reward quality of food. *Science* 201: 262–264, 1978.
31. Dackis CA, Gold MS: Bromocriptine as a treatment of cocaine abuse. *Lancet* 1: 1151–1152, 1985.
32. Colpaert FC, Niemegeers CJE, Janssen PAJ: Discriminative stimulus properties of cocaine: Neuropharmacological characteristics as derived from stimulus generalization experiments. *Pharm Biochem & Behav* 10: 535–546, 1979.
33. Gold MS, Dackis CA, Pottash ALC, et al.: Naltrexone, opiate addiction, and endorphins. *Med Res Rev* 2(3): 211–246, 1982.
34. Gold MS, Pottash ALC, Annitto WJ, et al.: Cocaine withdrawal: efficacy of tyrosine. *Soc Neurosci Abstr* 9: 157, 1983.
35. Dackis CA, Estroff TW, Sweeney DR, Pottash ALC, Gold MS: Specificity of the TRH test for major depression in patients with serious cocaine abuse. *Am J Psychiatry* 142: 1097–1099, 1985.
36. Dackis CA, Gold MS: Neurotransmitter and neuroendocrine abnormalities associated with cocaine use. *Psych Med*, 1986 (in press).

Cocaine Abuse and Dependence: The Scope of the Problem

Edward Gottheil, MD, PhD

ABSTRACT. The dramatic increase in cocaine use over the past 20 years has been of epidemic proportions. Cocaine is an extremely attractive and captivating drug that is a powerful reinforcer, induces strong psychological dependence and produces marked adverse behavioral changes. These characteristics, for planning purposes, would seem to suggest that the problem will continue to expand in scope. What we still do not know is the extent to which this increased use translates into a need for treatment. If as few as 10% of the users become problem users, as occurs with alcohol, we may be faced with a tremendous surge in demand for services such as occurred in the late sixties and for which we are similarly unprepared. We need to launch a major national effort to gain much more basic epidemiologic data, monitor the course of the epidemic, and support the development of new preventive and treatment approaches specifically tailored to cocaine, based on its particular advantages and disadvantages and the characteristics of its user population.

Twenty years ago, there were about 10,000 cocaine users in the United States. Ten years ago, there were about 100,000. Current estimates range from five to over 20 million.[1,2] There is documentation of increasing use by high school seniors.[3] From 1975 to 1982, there were more than five fold increases in the number of cocaine-related emergency room visits, admissions to drug treatment programs, and deaths.[4]

PERCEIVED ADVANTAGES

Some of the benefits commonly attributed to cocaine may help account for its tremendous increase in popularity. For example, a

---

Edward Gottheil is Professor of Psychiatry and Human Behavior at Thomas Jefferson University.

pleasurable, subjective quality of experience is described which provides drive, sparkle, and energy without a feeling of being drugged. Freud, writing about his use of the drug, commented on the exhilaration, alertness, vigor, and feeling of self-control that occurred and which seemed so normal that it was difficult to believe it was drug induced.[5] Aleister Crowley was more lyrical in his description of the effects of cocaine.

> The melancholy vanishes, the eyes shine, the wan mouth smiles. Almost manly vigor returns or seems to return. At least faith, hope and love throng very eagerly to the dance; all that was lost is found . . . To one the drug may bring liveliness, to another languor, to another creative force, to another tireless energy, to another glamour, and yet another, lust. But each in his own way is happy. Think of it! The man is happy.[6]

Cocaine is believed to have aphrodisiac properties and to be nonaddictive. It is also felt to be safe, especially when taken intranasally, and, as compared to other drug usage, does not result in lung CA, holes in arms, hangovers, or burned out brain cells. In addition, its exotic history, high price, and apparent respectability has made it a high status drug.

DISADVANTAGES

Each of these perceived advantages is either fleeting or illusory. With continued use, the early positive effects soon give way to more long term negative effects and consequences (Table 1).

Quality of the Experience

Depending on the mode of administration, peak euphoria and blood level occurs in 5 to 30 minutes and is followed by a let-down feeling. The let-down becomes more intense as one proceeds from one episode to another becoming characterized by irritability, restlessness, depression, anxiety, and, as might be expected, a craving for more drug. As frequency and quantity of use escalate, there may be insomnia, lack of appetite, weight loss, jitteriness, and the use of other drugs to combat these feelings. Suspiciousness is

Table I

Effects of Cocaine Usage

Perceived Advantages	Observed Disadvantages
A. Pleasurable experience	A. Dysphoric consequences
B. Aphrodisiac	B. Sexual dysfunction is more common.
C. Non-addictive	C. Overwhelming psychological dependence.
D. Safe	D. Narrow margin of safety. Medical and psychiatric disorders.
E. High status drug	E. Typical user is not of high socioeconomic status.

frequent and troublesome often leading to aggressive and hostile behavior. Hallucinations, especially of the tactile and visual variety, are common and frightening and may eventuate in a syndrome resembling an acute paranoid schizophrenia.

Crowley has also described the consequences of continuing use of cocaine.

But to one who abuses cocaine for his pleasure, nature soon speaks, and is not heard. The nerves weary of the constant stimulation; they need rest and food. There is a point at which the jaded horse no longer answers whip and spurs. He stumbles, falls a quivering heap, gasps out his life. . . So perishes the slave of cocaine. With every nerve clamoring, all he can do is to renew the lash of the poison. The pharmaceutical effect is over; the toxic effect accumulates. The nerves become insane. The victim begins to have hallucinations . . . and alas! The power of the drug diminishes with fearful pace. The doses wax; the pleasures wane. Side issues, invisible at first, arise; they are like devils with flaming pitchforks in their hands.[6]

Sexual Effect

Like alcohol, cocaine in occasional, small amounts may promote a feeling of well-being and enhance sexual interest, whereas large amounts result in difficulty. The cocaine high peaks quickly and is replaced by fatigue and depression which are not especially compatible with sexual performance. Higher doses of the drug do not prolong the euphoric feeling but merely increase the blood level producing increased pulse rate, blood pressure and tension which are most likely to result in less interest and less potency. If the cocaine is not pure and contains narcotics as adulterants, these drugs may also disturb sexual function. In sum, while cocaine may briefly result in heightened interest and even performance, it requires delicate timing which is not usually the strong suit of individuals who turn to stimulant drugs. More frequently cocaine is associated with sexual dysfunction.

An analysis of the responses of 500 individuals who called the national cocaine hotline is relevant.[7] The effects described by the callers as most desired included: mood elevation, increased drive, energy, and mental capacity, enhanced sociability, and sexual arousal. In contrast, what was reported was depression, irritability, cognitive deficits, being overwhelmed with problems, lacking in motivation, and an absence of sex drive. It might also be noted that approximately 10% of the callers reported a cocaine-related suicide attempt.

Tolerance and Addiction

When cocaine is repeatedly administered to animals, certain of its effects, such as those on heart rate, respiratory rate, and the E.E.G., are noted to decrease indicating tolerance, whereas other effects, such as those on locomotor activity and stereotyped behavior, increase indicating sensitization. In humans, tolerance also occurs to some of the effects of cocaine and withdrawal results in some physiological changes, however, there is no dramatic withdrawal syndrome such as one sees with alcohol, barbiturates, or narcotics. One can debate about the extent to which physiological dependency occurs, but the issue is really of little consequence since the overwhelming problem is the degree of psychological dependency and craving deriving from the extremely strong reinforcing power of this drug.

In experiments in which animals are trained to press a lever to obtain a cocaine reward, it has been found necessary to restrict the amount of total cocaine available by limiting the size of the dose, the number of doses, or the duration of the experiment. If not restricted, and given free access to the drug, rhesus monkeys, for example, go through bouts of severe intoxication leading to restlessness, profound anorexia, stereotyped movements, piloerection, tremor, self-mutilation, grand mal convulsions, and even death.[8] Findings with rats are similar. They will lever press until they die, leaving food and water untouched.[9] As an illustration of the relative reinforcing power of cocaine, rats would press a bar 250 times to obtain caffeine, 4,000 times to obtain heroin, and 10,000 times to obtain cocaine.[10]

The situation is not that different in the human. Most cocaine binges do not terminate until the individual is completely exhausted or has run out of cocaine.

Safety

Psychological dependency, increasing use, craving, depression, insomnia, weight loss, hallucinations, paranoia, and suicidal attempts do not seem pleasurable or safe. In addition, the drug is characterized by a narrow margin of safety, overdoses occur, and the number of cocaine-related deaths is steadily increasing even when taken by the intranasal route. The cocaine user is often unaware that following administration the blood level increases rapidly to a peak but then decreases slowly and that the let-down feeling and desire for more drug occurs shortly after the peak when the blood concentration is still almost at peak level. Thus, when successive lines are snorted, the blood level increases stepwise and can easily and in a short time reach levels comparable to those obtained with I.V. administration.

Status

The high cost of the drug contributes to its allure, but with regular use quickly becomes burdensome. The "king", "caviar", or "Cadillac" of drugs is really much more expensive than anything it is compared with including gold dust. At $100 per gram or $3,000 per ounce, a $30,000 per year habit is common and can go much higher. The financial drain and the cognitive and behavioral effects of such a regular habit impair occupational functioning even as the need for more drug continues to increase. The relentless pursuit of cocaine and money predominates as family, friends, and jobs are lost. Lying, cheating, stealing, and dealing may become necessary as the course comes more and more to resemble the familiar one of the garden variety "street" addict. This is quite a different picture from the one usually presented of the glamorous cocaine user.

We conducted a survey of physicians in several specialties practicing in the Philadelphia area to determine the number and characteristics of cocaine users they had seen during a one-month period. The findings that emerged from the survey did not support the commonly held conception of the cocaine user as an older, high income, successful entrepreneur or professional. Rather, the typical cocaine user seen by physicians in the Philadephia area was a young male in his twenties, of low or middle income, who used many illicit drugs in addition to cocaine, and who had been using them for a considerable period of time.

DISCUSSION

The dramatic increase in cocaine use over the past 20 years has been of epidemic proportions. Indeed, one measure of the scope of the cocaine problem is that the number of users is now estimated to exceed 20 million. What we do not know, however, is the extent to which this use translates into a demand or need for services.

Marijuana users rarely present themselves for treatment. LSD users formerly and PCP users currently come to attention more frequently because they more often experience acute emergent conditions. Alcoholic and narcotic users fall somewhere in between. The treatment use patterns of cocaine users are still unknown but presumably will most closely resemble those of alcoholic patients.

What is probably most needed at the present time is a major national effort to gain much more basic epidemiologic data. We need to know not only how many people are using but who they are, how much they are using, what the use patterns are and how they progress over time; what proportion remain recreational users and what proportion escalate through frequent use to regular use to problem use and how much time elapses between these different stages. Once into problem use, how many are able to return to recreational use or no use, how many die, how many are treated successfully, how many turn to other drugs?

The future course of the cocaine epidemic remains unclear. We do know that we are faced with an extremely attractive and captivating drug that induces strong psychological dependence and produces marked adverse behavioral changes. These characteristics, for planning purposes, would seem to suggest that the problem will continue to expand in scope. The course thus far is not compatible with the hope that it would merely be a passing fad as was the case with LSD. It may be that most individuals will be found able to remain recreational users and will not constitute a significant public health problem. This seems most unlikely. Cocaine, as different from marijuana, is a most powerful reinforcer, produces strong craving and dependency, and may often result in depression, anxiety, suspiciousness, aggressive behavior, hallucinations and even death. Could the drug be used in moderation in this society as it has been in South America? This, too, seems unlikely given the great differences in the two cultures and the presence in this country of a 30 billion dollar illicit drug industrial complex involved in the merchandising and marketing of cocaine.[11]

If, like alcohol, as few as 10% of the users become problem users, we may expect that there are or will be a minimum of 2 million problem users in the country. Unlike alcohol, however, cocaine is extremely expensive, and it may be expected that a much greater proportion of cocaine users than alcoholics will be unable to obtain adequate supplies of their drug and become desperately in need of treatment, creating a greater demand for services than is true of the current populations of either alcohol or narcotic abusers. We have not seen this yet and long lines of patients awaiting admission to treatment programs have not been forming, although there are some reports that this is starting to occur in California. Some have suggested that the progression from first use to regular use to problem use takes about five years. Perhaps seven or ten or twelve years are required. The question is whether we are going to experience a tremendous surge in demand for services such as occurred in the late sixties and for which we are similarly unprepared.

We need epidemiologic data from carefully selected, appropriate, national samples. Our current efforts at prevention did not prevent this epidemic and we may need to develop new approaches specifically tailored to cocaine and based on its particular advantages and disadvantages and the characteristics of its user population. Treatment outcome studies are sorely lacking. Do any of our treatments help and are some better than others for particular groups of patients? We may need to develop new treatments searching possibly for a new antabuse or methadone, special types of self-help groups, or a particular therapeutic milieu.

Since we do not have a National Institute of Cocaine Abuse, the number of new grants to be supported in the currently proposed budget is limited, and our needs for epidemiologic, prevention, treatment evaluation, and new treatment studies are enormous, the scope of the cocaine problem looms very large indeed.

REFERENCES

1. Research on Mental Illness and Addictive Disorders: Progress and Prospects. Report of the Board on Mental Health and Behavioral Medicine of the Institute of Medicine, National Academy of Sciences. Washington, D.C.: National Academy Press, 1984.
2. National Institute on Drug Abuse: National Household Survey on Drug Abuse, 1982. Washington, D.C.: U.S. Department of Health and Human Services, Alcohol, Drug Abuse, and Mental Health Administration, 1983.
3. Johnson LD, O'Malley PM, Bachman JG. Drugs and American High School Students 1975–1983. Washington, D.C.: U.S. Department of Health and Human Services, Alcohol, Drug Abuse, and Mental Health Administration, 1984.
4. National Institute on Drug Abuse: Data from the Drug Abuse Warning Network, Series G, Number 12. Washington, D.C.: U.S. Department of Health and Human Services, Alcohol, Drug Abuse, and Mental Health Administration, 1983.
5. Freud S. Uber coca (1884). In: Byck R, ed. Cocaine Papers by Sigmund Freud. New York: Stonehill, 1974:48–73.
6. Siegel RK. Cocaine: Recreational use and intoxication. In: Petersen RC, Stillman RC, eds. Cocaine. Natl Inst Drug Abuse Res Monogr Ser 13, Washington, D.C.: U.S. Government Printing Office, 1977:119–136.
7. Washton AM, Gold MS. Chronic cocaine abuse: Evidence for adverse effects on health and functioning. Psychiatric Annals. 1984: 14:733–746.
8. Johanson CE, Balster RL, Bonese K. Self administration of psychomotor stimulant drugs: The effects of unlimited access. Pharmacol Biochem Behav 1976; 4:45–51.
9. Woods J. Behavioral effects of cocaine in animals. In: Petersen RC, Stillman RC, eds. Cocaine. Natl Inst Drug Abuse Res Monogr Ser. 13 Washington, D.C.: U.S. Government Printing Office, 1977:63–95.
10. Spotts JV, Shontz FC. The Lifestyles of Nine American Cocaine Users: Trips to the Land of Cockaigne. Natl Inst Drug Abuse Res 16 Washington, D.C.: U.S. Government Printing Office, 1976.
11. Demarest M. Cocaine: Middle class high. Time, July 6, 1981:56–63.

Recent Trends in Cocaine Abuse: A View from the National Hotline, "800-COCAINE"

Arnold M. Washton, PhD
Mark S. Gold, MD

ABSTRACT. A series of research surveys of callers to the "800-COCAINE" National Hotline over the past three years has revealed shifting patterns of cocaine use in the U.S. In addition to showing the geographic spread of cocaine use to virtually all parts of the country, the surveys provide evidence of increased cocaine use among women, adolescents, minorities, and lower socioeconomic groups. Increases have also been seen in individual levels of cocaine consumption, the popularity of freebase smoking, concomitant use of other drugs, cocaine-related automobile accidents, and the use of cocaine in the workplace. Despite inherent limitations, data from the Hotline are highly consistent with large-scale government surveys and predictive of clinical trends.

INTRODUCTION AND BACKGROUND

In its first two years of operation, the National Cocaine Hotline, "800-COCAINE," has received more than 1.2 million calls, often at a rate exceeding 1,200 per day. The calls have come from virtually every state and geographic region in the U.S. Approximately 60% of the calls come from cocaine and other drug users: the remaining 40% come from concerned family members, friends, and profes-

Dr. Washton is Director of Addiction Research and Treatment at The Regent Hospital in New York City and at Stony Lodge Hospital in Ossining, NY. He is also Research Director of the National Cocaine Hotline, "800-COCAINE," at Fair Oaks Hospital in Summit, NJ.

Dr. Gold is Director of Research at Fair Oaks Hospital in Summit, NJ and in Delray Beach, FL; The Regent Hospital in New York City; and Stony Lodge Hospital in Ossining, NY. He is also Founder of the National Cocaine Hotline.

sionals seeking help or advice for a drug user. Twenty-four hours each day, the Hotline provides immediate access to information, advice, and a treatment referral (if needed) anywhere in the 50 states. The Hotline center, based at Fair Oaks Hospital in New Jersey, is staffed by a team of trained and experienced substance abuse counselors, many of whom are themselves recovering cocaine addicts.

In addition to providing easy access to information and assistance, the Hotline has served to heighten public awareness about the growing epidemic of cocaine use in the U.S. The enormous volume of calls in itself has made it difficult to ignore just how widespread and pervasive the problem has become. The Hotline and its survey findings have received a great deal of media attention. This has helped to stimulate public concern about the cocaine epidemic in the U.S. and to prompt further inquiry by health professionals and by government officials.

The establishment of the National Hotline was preceded by a local New York City "cocaine helpline" initiated by the first author (AMW) in January 1983. To our knowledge this was the first such telephone hotline for cocaine abusers in the U.S. or elsewhere. This initial hotline experience revealed, in perhaps the most dramatic way up to that time, that there were large numbers of employed middle-class cocaine abusers who had become severely dependent on the drug and were having great difficulty finding professional help. They were being told by private clinicians and by drug abuse experts that cocaine was not addictive, that no detoxification was required, and that no formal treatment was either necessary or available. It was clear from the reports of these early hotline callers that neither the public drug abuse treatment programs which tend to be concerned mainly with hard-core heroin addiction, nor private clinicians who are typically unfamiliar with the treatment of drug addiction, were equipped to deal with what appeared to be a large but previously unrecognized population of cocaine abusers desperately trying to seek help. The callers sensed that they had become addicted to cocaine, but their observations were being refuted by professionals and contradicted what they had been told previously about the drug's apparent harmlessness. Many of these callers asked: "How can I be addicted to a drug that is supposedly non-addictive?" "Is there something especially wrong with me—are others having this problem?"

In addition to uncovering these phenomena, the New York hotline served as a vehicle for collecting research data. From among the 200–300 calls per day, a random sample of 55 callers was selected to participate in an anonymous telephone research interview lasting 30–40 minutes. The interview was based on an extensive research questionnaire that was designed to collect information on the demographics of the callers, their history and current patterns of cocaine use, their use of other drugs, the effects and side effects of cocaine, and any negative consequences of cocaine use on their health and functioning. The results of this survey[1] provided clearcut and dramatic evidence of compulsive patterns of cocaine use associated with a wide range of medical, psychological, and social problems. The typical respondent in this random sample was a white, middle-class male, 25–35 years old, with no prior history of drug addiction or psychiatric illness. Nearly all said they felt addicted to cocaine and unable to stop using the drug despite numerous adverse effects.

When the National Hotline was subsequently established in May 1983, it became clear that the cocaine epidemic was not only in New York: it was nationwide. The phones began to ring incessantly almost from the very first instant that the Hotline went into operation. At first the calls came mainly from the New York City area and other locations in the northeast since these were the places where the Hotline initially received the most media attention and publicity. As news about the Hotline spread to other parts of the country, the volume of calls from those areas started to increase accordingly. Within the first three months the Hotline had received calls from more than 37 different states in the U.S. Forced by a rapidly soaring volume of calls to expand its operating hours to 24 hours per day and increase its number of incoming phone lines, the Hotline became a dramatic example of how serious and widespread the cocaine problem had become without either the public or the professional community being sufficiently aware of it.

The National Hotline afforded unprecedented access to large numbers of cocaine abusers who would otherwise not be available for study by traditional methods. The research questionnaire constructed for the earlier New York hotline was expanded[2] and a series of national surveys were begun. To date, we have surveyed more than 3,500 callers in our attempt to obtain information about different aspects of the cocaine problem. Our Hotline studies provide one of the few available sources of information about changes in the cocaine epidemic; i.e., trends or shifts in patterns of cocaine use in the U.S. By comparing surveys taken from nationwide samples at different points in time, the Hotline has helped to detect some of the major trends in cocaine abuse over the past two and one-half years. The results of our surveys have been published in several reports.[2,3,4] In this article, we will present some of our major findings with particular emphasis on changing patterns and trends in cocaine abuse. Our discussion will include the first national survey conducted in 1983 and its comparison with an updated survey conducted in 1985, as well as surveys that have focused on the problems of cocaine use in adolescents and cocaine use in the workplace.

There are some important methodological problems that may limit the interpretation of our Hotline data. For one, we are dealing with a skewed sample of respondents. One might expect that Hotline callers would include primarily those cocaine users whose problem is more severe that others who do not seek assistance. There is no doubt that our Hotline callers do not represent all cocaine users, and may particularly exclude those in the earlier stages of use and those who have not already experienced significant drug-related problems. (This problem will also apply to any study of individuals who apply for treatment and/or those who are already enrolled in a treatment program.) Although our samples are admittedly biased, it should be noted that the levels of cocaine use reported among our survey respondents span an extremely wide range and that all of the surveys do in fact include many individuals who were calling the Hotline not for a treatment referral or because they felt that they had a problem with cocaine, but for information or to satisfy their curiosity. Still, our findings cannot be generalized to all individuals who use cocaine. Secondly, the geographic distribution of respondents is not representative of a true cross-section of cocaine users in the U.S. The volume of calls from a particular geographic area of the country is affected greatly by amount of media attention the Hotline receives in that area at a given point in time and its temporal relationship to the data collection process. Lastly, one must take into consideration that our research interview was conducted entirely by telephone with anonymous callers. While on the one hand the freedom to report anonymously is exactly what has made the surveys possible, the accuracy of the callers' responses and their tendency to either exaggerate or downplay the extent of their drug use and its resulting consequences can be questioned. Itcan be noted, however, that on the many occasions where a Hotline caller has subsequently come in for a more extensive clinical assessment, we have noted no large discrepancies in the relevant information. Nonetheless, this potential limitation exists and should not be overlooked.

Despite these limitations, we have been encouraged by the ofttimes close correspondence between many of our survey findings and those of large-scale government surveys[5] that have used sophisticated sampling and interview techniques. A comparison of our findings with these other surveys is discussed at the end of the paper.

NATIONAL SURVEY: 1983

Our first national survey[4] was based on a random sample of 500 callers to the Hotline during its initial three months of operation, May through July, 1983. The sample included callers from 37 different states across the U.S. with the majority being from New York, New Jersey, California and Florida, which collectively represented 63% of the entire sample. Each caller voluntarily consented to an anonymous 30–40 minute telephone interview in which the research questionnaire was administered. This study amplified and extended the earlier New York survey by Washton and Tatarsky.[1] It provided the first multi-state demographic profile of cocaine users in the U.S., and more fully described the true nature of cocaine dependency and its consequences.

1. Demographic Profile

The average age of the 500 respondents was 30 years, with most being between 25 and 40 years old at the time of their call to the hotline. Some were as young as 16 and as old as 78. Sixty-seven percent were male, 33% were female. The overwhelming majority (85%) were white; 15% were Black or Hispanic. Many were well-educated, on average having completed just over 14 years of schooling. The sample included many college graduates, degreed professionals, and highly skilled business executives and technicians. Forty percent had incomes over $25,000 per year.

2. Cocaine and Other Drug Use

The respondents had begun their use of cocaine on average 4.9 years before calling the Hotline, and over 90% had started with intranasal use ("snorting"). At the time of their call, 61% were taking the drug intranasally, 21% were freebase smoking, and 18% were intravenous users. About half the sample was using cocaine daily, at a street cost of $75 to $150 per gram. Many reported "binge" patterns of use in which they used the drug continuously for two or three days at a time until their supply of the drug, money, or physical energy was totally exhausted. Some said they used the drug only on weekends. On average they were using about 6 grams per week, although this ranged from 1 to 32 grams per week. They said they had been spending an average of $637 per week for cocaine during the week before they called the Hotline, with a range from about $100 to $3,200. The vast majority of callers (80%) said that when the cocaine high wore off, they felt depressed, irritable, restless, and drained of energy—a rebound dysphoric reaction commonly referred to as the cocaine "crash." The importance of the "crash" lies in the fact that 68% of the respondents said that in order to alleviate the unpleasant aftereffects of cocaine they were led to abuse other drugs such as alcohol, sleeping pills, tranquilizers, or opiates. This finding revealed that cocaine abuse is likely to promote polydrug abuse and dependence. Many of the callers had become multiply dependent on a combination of cocaine, alcohol, and tranquilizers.

3. Addiction and Dependency

The questionnaire included a series of items to probe the issue of drug dependency and addiction. Callers were asked to indicate which, if any, of the items characterized their involvement with cocaine. Their replies provide clear evidence of the dependence-producing ability of the drug and its ability to dominate the user even in the face of extreme negative consequences. Overall, 61% said they felt addicted to cocaine; 83% said they could not turn down the drug when it was available; 73% said they had lost control and could not limit their cocaine use; 67% said they had been unable to stop using cocaine except for brief periods lasting no longer than one month. Overhalf the respondents said that cocaine had become more important to them than food, sex, recreational activities, social relationships, and job or career. Although it had become clear that cocaine use was impairing their functioning, most said that they feared feeling distressed and unable to function properly without the drug.

4. Drug-Related Consequences

Their compulsion to continue using cocaine despite serious adverse effects became even more clearly evident from the questionnaire items on drug-related consequences to health and functioning. This section of the questionnaire included a total of 59 items on physical, psychological, and social problems associated with cocaine use. Over 90% of the respondents reported five or more adverse effects that they attributed to their cocaine use. The five leading physical problems were chronic insomnia (82%), chronic fatigue (76%), severe headaches (60%), nasal and sinus infections (58%), and disrupted sexual functioning (55%). Other serious physical problems included cocaine-induced brain seizures with loss of consciousness reported by 14% of the sample, and nausea and vomiting reported by 39%. The leading psychological problems were depression, anxiety, and irritability, each reported by more than 80% of the sample. Paranoia, loss of interest in non-drug related activities, difficulty concentrating, and loss of non-drug using friends were each reported by more than 60%. Nine percent reported a cocaine-induced suicide attempt. Numerous personal and social problems were also reported. For example, 45% said they had stolen money from their employers and from family or friends to support their cocaine habit. Most were in debt having spent all of their monetary assets on cocaine. Some had mortgaged their home, lost their business or profession, squandered their inheritance or trust fund, or sold their valuables for cocaine. Thirty-six percent said they had dealt drugs to support their cocaine habit; 26% reported marital/relationship problems ending in separation or divorce; 17% had lost a job due to cocaine; 12% had been arrested for a drug-related crime of dealing or possession of cocaine; 11% reported a cocaine-related automobile accident.

5. Route of Administration

It is commonly believed that people who use cocaine by snorting it are immune to becoming dependent on the drug or from suffering serious adverse consequences. Our earlier clinical experience did not support this view nor did the large numbers of intranasal users who were calling the Hotline and reporting serious problems.[3] We therefore made a special effort to examine our survey data for a comparison between the different methods of use.[4] We found that intranasal users reported patterns and consequences of cocaine use similar to those of freebase and IV users. The incidence and types of con- sequences reported by each group of users were comparable to one another, with one major difference: the freebase and IV users tended to show greater disruption of psychosocial functioning and were more likely to report nearly all of the most serious ill effects. For example, FB and IV users reported higher rates of cocaine-related brain seizures, automobile accidents, job loss, and extreme paranoia. This finding may have been at least partly due to the higher dosages of cocaine used by the FB and IV groups. Intranasal users who reported comparably high levels of use also reported comparably serious adverse effects. The data suggested that possibly another important difference between the different methods of cocaine use is the speed at which the user becomes addicted. Intranasal users typically reported a rather long period of occasional non-problematic use, sometimes 2–4 years, before becoming dependent on the drug. Those who started out with FB or IV use or those who later switched to these methods after an initial period of snorting cocaine, said that their drug use had reached problematic levels almost immediately—relatively few described their FB or IV use, even in its beginning stages, as "recreational" or non-problematic. Most felt that they were overcome almost immediately by irresistible drug cravings.

NATIONAL SURVEYS: 1983 vs. 1985

Table 1 compares selected results of the 1983 survey with a similar survey conducted almost two years later in 1985. These data reveal a number of significant shifts in patterns of cocaine use, as outlined below.

1. Geographic Shifts

The proportion of Hotline calls from southern and midwestern regions of the U.S. has increased significantly, although the absolute number of calls remain highest from the northeast and western regions of the country. This finding indicates that cocaine use has spread to virtually all areas of the U.S., including many small towns

Table I
HOTLINE SURVEYS: 1983 vs. 1985

Each survey is based on a random sample of 500 callers during a
three-month time period: May-July 1983 and January-March 1985.

	1983	1985
Origin of calls:		
Northeast	47%	32%
Midwest	11%	23%
West	33%	22%
South	9%	23%
Demographics:		
Males	67%	58%
Females	33%	42%
Whites	85%	64%
Black/Hispanic	15%	36%
Average Age	30 yr	27 yr
Adolescents	1%	7%
Yearly Income:		
$0-25,000	60%	73%
over $25,000	40%	27%
Cocaine Use:		
Consumption	6.5 gm/wk	7.2 gm/wk
Expenditure	$637	$535
Intranasal	61%	52%
Freebase	21%	30%
Intravenous	18%	18%
Use of other drugs to alleviate cocaine side effects:	68%	87%
Auto accident on cocaine:	11%	19%
Use of cocaine at work:	42%	74%

and rural areas which in 1983 were thought to be largely exempt from
the cocaine epidemic. We continue to receive calls on the Hotline
from many sparsely populated areas in the U.S., including small
towns in Wyoming, Montana, Mississippi, New Mexico, Alabama,

and others. Large cities and adjoining suburbs in the northeast, California, and Florida continue to show the highest absolute volume of calls.

2. Demographic Shifts

The profile of Hotline callers has changed substantially since 1983 when most callers were white middle/upper class employed males between the ages of 25 and 35. With the continuing spread of cocaine use over the past two years, it appears that a broader cross-section of the American population has become involved in this phenomenon. As a result, no single demographic profile accurately describes the majority of cocaine users: there is no longer a "typical" user. The data in Table 1 indicate increasing cocaine use among women, minority groups, lower-income groups, and adolescents. The major demographic shifts can be summarized as follows:

A. Women

In 1983, women cocaine abusers comprised about one-third of the randomly-sampled callers to the Hotline. In 1985, they comprise nearly one-half of the callers. Our more detailed surveys of women callers reveal that the vast majority (87%) are introduced to cocaine by a male companion and often receive "gifts" of cocaine from men indicative of how the drug has become incorporated into social relationships. On average, women report using less cocaine than men and are less likely to resort to drug dealing as a way to support their use. However, women are more likely than men to report extreme depression due to chronic cocaine use and to exchange sexual "favors" for the drug.

B. Minority and Lower-Income Groups

The proportion of black and hispanic callers has more than doubled since 1983. Similarly, more callers now report earning less than $25,000 per year.

C. Adolescents

The average age of callers has decreased, reflecting the spreading use of cocaine among younger users including adolescents, college students, and other young adults. For adolescents ages 13–19 there has been a sevenfold increase in the percentage of Hotline calls since 1983. A more detailed study of adolescent callers is described later in this article.

3. Levels of Cocaine Use

The surveys indicate that levels of cocaine use have increased, as shown by the callers self-reported estimates of weekly consumption. There has also been an increasing tendency for users to shift from snorting cocaine to freebase smoking. The data further indicate that the price of cocaine on the illicit market has dropped considerably from an average of approximately $98/gm in 1983 to about $75/gm in 1985.

4. Concomitant Use of Other Drugs

Our surveys show an increasing problem of polydrug abuse among current cocaine abusers. With increasing levels of cocaine consumption, users say they are more likely to resort to other drugs and alcohol in order to relieve the unpleasant side effects of cocaine. Abuse of alcohol and sedative-hypnotic drugs appears to be the rule rather than the exception among current cocaine abusers.

5. Automobile Accidents

Cocaine-related automobile accidents reported by Hotline callers have nearly doubled since 1983. In 1985, nearly one-fifth of all callers said they had had at least one automobile accident resulting in personal injury or property damage while under the influence of cocaine or a combination of cocaine and other drugs. The opposing effects of stimulants and depressants that differ with regard to the onset and duration of their actions appears to create an especially dangerous situation. Because cocaine's short-term stimulant effects temporarily mask the depressant effects of alcohol, the cocaine user is able to consume a large quantity of alcohol and initially not feel the intoxicating effects of the alcohol that might otherwise lead them to refrain from driving. When the cocaine wears off in only 20–30 minutes, the driver may suddenly become severely intoxicated or even stuperous from the alcohol with resulting gross and unexpected impairment of driving ability.

6. Cocaine Use in the Workplace

The percentage of callers who say they use cocaine at work increased sharply from 42% in 1983 to 74% in 1985. A more detailed survey of cocaine use in the workplace is presented later in this article.

ADOLESCENT COCAINE USE

Our surveys continue to show dramatic increases in cocaine use by adolescents. In a specific survey of adolescent cocaine users,[6] we interviewed 100 randomly-selected Hotline callers who were between the ages of 13 and 19. The interview included a structured research questionnaire requiring a 30–40 minute telephone interview.

Survey Results

A descriptive profile of the adolescent sample is shown in Table 2. Most were white male high school students in the 11th or 12th grade, with many from urban and suburban middle-class families. The time lag between snorting their first "line" of cocaine and evidence of cocaine-related disruption of functioning which lead them to call the Hotline averaged 1.5 years as contrasted with over 4 years in adult survey samples. Most were snorting cocaine although 12% had switched to more intensified methods of use. Nearly every subject reported multiple, combination drug use. Cocaine was often combined with or followed immediately by use of marijuana, alcohol, and sedative-hypnotic drugs, usually to counteract the unpleasant cocaine side effects. Most said that they were purchasing drugs from school mates and older users or dealers, often in or around school premises.

A wide range of cocaine-related medical, social, psychiatric, and school problems were reported by the adolescent respondents. School performance was reported to have suffered considerably because of the continuing cocaine use and its resulting problems. Seventy-five percent had missed days of school; 69% said their grades had dropped significantly; 48% had experienced disciplinary problems due to drug-related disruption of mood and behavior; and

Table 2
ADOLESCENT COCAINE ABUSERS
(N=100)

Demographics:		Current use:	
Males	65%	Consumption	1.4 gm/wk
Whites	83%	Expenditure	$95/wk
Average age	16.2 yr	Intranasal	88%
Avg education	11.4 yr	Freebase	10%
		Intravenous	2%
First use:			
Time before call	1.5 yr	Use of other drugs to	
Intranasal	100%	relieve cocaine side effects:	
		Marijuana	92%
		Alcohol	85%
		Sedatives	64%
		Heroin	4%

31% had been expelled for cocaine-related difficulties. To support their escalating drug use, 44% had been selling drugs; 31% were stealing from family, friends, or employer; and 62% were using lunch or travel money or income from a part-time job to buy drugs. Among the most serious drug-related consequences were: cocaine-induced brain seizures with loss of consciousness (19%), automobile accidents (13%), suicide attempts (14%), and violent behavior (27%). Similar to adult users, common complaints included: insomnia, fatigue, depression, irritability, short-temper, paranoia, headaches, nasal and sinus problems, poor appetite, weight loss, memory and concentration problems, and heart palpitations. In most cases, loss of interest in non-drug using friends, family activities, and sports or hobbies were also reported. Nearly every subject said that the only limit on their cocaine use was money: if they had more money they would use more cocaine. The results of this survey show that adolescents do indeed have sufficient access to cocaine to become serious abusers and that their vulnerability to the dependence-producing properties of the drug and disruption of functioning may be greater than that of adults.

COCAINE USE IN THE WORKPLACE

The problem of drug use in the workplace is a matter of rapidly escalating concern not only to employers but to society at large. The broadening scope of this problem in terms of its negative impact on individual health and safety as well as on the nation's economy are just starting to become recognized. It seemed to us that if most cocaine users are employed, then there must be a great deal of cocaine and other drug use that occurs in the workplace. To our knowledge, no previous attempts had been made to study this phenomenon by actually interviewing drug-using employees. We took a random sample of 227 employed cocaine abusers who called the Hotline and consented to a research interview concerning drug use on the job.

Survey Results

The demographic profile of these drug-using employees was as follows: 70% were male; 61% were white; 53% were 20–29 years old, 40% were 30–39 years old, and 7% were 40 years old or over; 67% earned under $25,000 per year, 32% earned $26–50,000, and 1% earned over $50,000. Their occupations included the following: automobile mechanic, attorney, stock broker, legal secretary, salesperson, real estate agent, airline flight attendant, dentist, nurse, optician, pharmacist, physician, laboratory technician, bank executive, prison guard, carpenter, electrician, office clerk, postal employee, public utility worker, security guard, computer programmer, retail store owner, pipe fitter, bus driver, and railway switchman.

Seventy-four percent said they used drugs at work. This includes respondents who said that they had self-administered drugs during working hours (or breaks) as well as those who had come to work while already under the influence of drugs. The types of drugs used at work were as follows: cocaine (83%), alcohol (39%), marijuana (33%), sedative-hypnotics (13%), and opiates (10%). (The total of these percentages exceed 100% because most subjects reported multiple drug use.) Sixty-four percent said that drugs were readily obtainable at their place of work and 44% said they had dealt drugs to fellow employees. Twenty-six percent reported being fired from at least one previous job because of drug-related problems; 39% feared that a raise in salary would lead to further escalation of their drug use. Eighteen percent said they had stolen money from co-workers in order to buy drugs and 20% reported having at least one drug-related accident on the job.

COMMENT

It is clear that cocaine abuse has grown from what appeared to be a relatively minor problem in the sixties and seventies to a major public health problem today. Government reports issued in 1973[7,8] concluded that problems associated with cocaine use did not appear to be significant and that few who used the drug actually sought professional help in drug abuse treatment programs or elsewhere. It was further stated that there had been no confirmed cases of cocaine overdose deaths. Unfortunately, these reports and others in the medical literature[9] have served to legitimize and fuel the myth that cocaine is harmless and nonaddictive. The apparent low rates of problematic cocaine use were probably more the result of the drug's high price and limited availability in the U.S. at that time rather than its presumed low abuse potential.

As seen from our Hotline surveys and other sources, the situation has changed drastically. Evidence of addictive patterns of cocaine use and wide-ranging adverse consequences is indisputable. The academic debates about whether or not cocaine is truly addicting will probably continue, but the behavioral evidence is already clear. Consistent with our Hotline experience, government surveys in more recent years, reviewed by Adams and Durell,[5] show that the prevalence of cocaine use in the U.S. has increased dramatically since the late seventies. Similarly, there have been significant increases in the medical consequences of cocaine use according to the government statistics on cocaine-related emergency room episodes, deaths, and admissions to government-sponsored drug abuse treatment programs.[10]

In addition to an overall increase in the prevalence of cocaine abuse and its health consequences, our Hotline surveys identify other noteworthy trends. Here too, our findings are consistent with government surveys.[5] The Hotline data show major demographic shifts in user profiles indicating increased cocaine use among women, minority groups, lower-income groups, and adolescents. It has become abundantly clear that cocaine use is no longer restricted primarily to white middle and upper-class adult males. A major contributor to the spreading use has been the increasing availability of cocaine supplies at reduced prices. This has made the drug more accessible to a much larger segment of the population. On average, a gram of cocaine is now cheaper than an ounce of marijuana in many places across the U.S. The greater accessibility to cocaine has no doubt also contributed to more intensified use among current users as reflected in the higher dosages reported by Hotline callers and the increasing popularity of freebase smoking—a method of administration that almost invariably leads to more compulsive, higher-dose use. A 1982 government report[10] indicated a dramatic increase in cocaine freebasing from 1% of treatment admissions in 1979 to almost 7% in 1982.

The greater tendency toward polydrug abuse reported by our Hotline callers is also supported by the 1982 government report[10] which stated that 82% of all primary cocaine abusers admitted to government treatment programs said they were experiencing at least one other concurrent drug problem. This phenomenon could be explained by the fact that as an individual's cocaine abuse intensifies so do the negative aftereffects of the cocaine, thus creating a greater need to alleviate these aftereffects with other substances.

The presumed safety of intranasal cocaine use has been challenged consistently in all of our surveys. Intranasal users continue to account for over 50% of callers to the Hotline and for the majority of treatment admissions for cocaine problems in our own programs and elsewhere. Consistent with our survey findings, other observations[11] indicate that both freebase smoking and intravenous use of cocaine are more likely to engender daily, compulsive use patterns than does intranasal use. Nonetheless, the potential dangers of snorting cocaine should not be underestimated. In addition to problems of addiction and drug-related dysfunction, there have been instances of death from intranasal cocaine verified by coroner's reports.[12]

One might hope that the current upsurge in cocaine use would be a short-lived, temporary phenomenon—a passing fad that would dissipate as quickly as it seemed to appear. Unfortunately, this seems highly unlikely. The current cocaine epidemic has already become too pervasive and indications are that it is still growing at a rate that would make rapid resolution of the problem all but impossible. The enormous profits of the illicit cocaine industry have resulted in increased production and supplies of the drug and a powerful motivation to continue making the drug available to as large a segment of the U.S. population as possible. (Cocaine problems are now starting to surface in other countries such as Great Britain and West Germany.) Since there is usually a time lag of about 4–5 years between the onset of cocaine use and its escalation to the point where the user is driven to seek help, the peak effects of the current epidemic in the U.S. may not be seen for quite a while. Although public education and other prevention efforts may help to discourage future experimentation, at present it appears that if supplies of the drug continue to increase while prices continue to decline, the current epidemic is likely to become even more widespread and intensified.

REFERENCES

1. Washton AM, Tatarsky A. Adverse effects of cocaine abuse. In LS Harris (Ed.) Problems of drug dependence, 1983. Washington, DC: US Gov't Printing Office, NIDA Research Monograph No. 44, pp. 247–254, 1984.

2. Gold MS. 800-Cocaine. New York: Bantam, 1984.

√3. Washton AM, Gold MS, Pottash AC. Intranasal cocaine addiction. Lancet 2, 1983; 1378 (letter).

4. Washton AM, Gold MS. Chronic cocaine abuse: evidence for adverse effects on health and functioning. Psychiatric Annals 1984; 14:733–743.

5. Adams EH, Durell J. Cocaine: a growing public health problem. In J Grabowski (Ed.) Cocaine: pharmacology, effects and treatment of abuse. NIDA Research Monograph No. 50. Washington, DC: US Gov't Printing Office, DHHS publication number (ADM)84–1326, pp. 9–4, 1984.

6. Washton AM, Gold MS, Pottash AC, Semlitz L. Adolescent cocaine abusers. Lancet 2, 1984; ll (letter).

7. National Commission on Marihuana and Drug Abuse. Drug Use in America: Problem in Perspective. Second Report of the National Commission on Marihuana and Drug Abuse. Washington, DC: National Institute on Drug Abuse, March, 1973.

8. Strategy Council on Drug Abuse. Federal Strategy for Drug Abuse and Drug Traffic Prevention 1973. Washington, DC: Supt of Docs, US Gov't Printing Office, 1973.

9. Van Dyke C, and Byck R. Cocaine. Scientific American 1982; 246: 128–141.

10. Kozel NJ, Crider RA, Adams EH. National surveillance of cocaine use and related health consequences. Centers for Disease Control, Atlanta, Georgia: DHHS publication number (CDC)82-8017. Also published in: Morbidity and Mortality Weekly Report No. 31. 1982; 20: 265–273.

11. Adams EH. Abuse/availability trends of cocaine in the United States. Drug Surveillance Reports, 1982; Volume 2. NIDA Division of Epidemiology and Statistical Reports, Rockville, Maryland.

√2. Wetli CV, Wright RK. Death caused by recreational cocaine use. JAMA 1979; 241: 2519–2522.

Trends in Prevalence and Consequences of Cocaine Use

Edgar H. Adams, MS
Joseph C. Gfroerer, BA
Beatrice A. Rouse, PhD
Nicholas J. Kozel, MS

ABSTRACT. A variety of data sources and research studies are used to examine changes in the prevalence of cocaine use and assess the population at risk. The issues of progression to more intensified use of cocaine and the use of other drugs in combination with cocaine are investigated. Consequences of cocaine use are discussed, as is the potential impact of changing routes of administration on both the frequency and severity of those consequences.

INTRODUCTION

Cocaine use in the United States was widespread in the late 19th and early 20th centuries when it was an ingredient in many patent medicines, tonics, and soft drinks. Between the 1930's and the late 60's, cocaine all but disappeared from the American scene. This downturn in cocaine use has been attributed to a number of factors including the Depression, restrictions on the importation, manufacture and distribution of cocaine as well as the introduction of amphetamines in 1932. The amphetamines were legal, available,

The authors are affiliated with the Division of Epidemiology and Statistical Analysis, National Institute on Drug Abuse, Public Health Service, Department of Health and Human Services. Address reprint requests to: Edgar H. Adams, Acting Director, Division of Epidemiology and Statistical Analysis, National Institute on Drug Abuse, Room 11A–55, 5600 Fishers Lane, Rockville, MD 20857.

The views expressed in this paper are those of the authors and are not meant to represent the official position of the National Institute on Drug Abuse or the Department of Health and Human Services.

The authors wish to express their appreciation to Marge Betts for her dedicated assistance in typing and formatting this report and to Betsy Slay, Lynne Schneider, Helen Lin, and Diane Reznikov for developing special computer tabulations used in preparing it.

49

and cheap, and, in addition, had a longer duration of action than cocaine.[1]

Although in the 1960's illicit drug use, and in particular marijuana use, spread throughout the younger population, cocaine use was not viewed as a major problem. By 1972, 14 percent of youth (age 12–17 yrs.) and 47.9 percent of young adults (age 18–25 yrs.) had tried marijuana, whereas the prevalence of lifetime cocaine use was 1.5 percent and 9.1 percent, respectively. The second report from the National Commission on Marihuana and Drug Abuse in 1973 stated that little social cost related to cocaine had been verified in this country. This was attributed to the normal route of administration, i.e., sniffing or "snorting," having fewer adverse consequences and to low prevalence of chronic use.[2] At the same time, the Strategy Council on Drug Abuse stated that morbidity associated with cocaine use did not appear to be great. They further stated that there were virtually no confirmed cocaine overdose deaths and that a negligible number seek medical help or seek the kind of treatment offered by specialized drug treatment programs.[3] At the time this assessment was essentially correct, given the information that was available.

INCIDENCE AND PREVALENCE OF COCAINE USE

Since the early 1970's, dramatic increases in cocaine use have been well documented. The number of people trying cocaine at least once (Lifetime Prevalence) has increased from 5.4 million in 1974 to 21.6 million in 1982.[4] The largest rate of increase on an annual basis took place between 1976 and 1977 when a 50 percent increase in lifetime prevalence was noted (Table 1). The number of current users (use in past 30 days) of cocaine increased from 1.6 million in

TABLE 1

Trends in Lifetime Prevalence (Ever Used) of Cocaine
1974-1982

(Number of persons in thousands)

1974	1976	1977	1979	1982
5,370	6,490	9,820	15,160	21,570

Source: NIDA, unpublished data from the National Survey on Drug Abuse

1977 to 4.3 million in 1979 and remained stable at about 4.2 million in 1982.[5]

Further examination of the data from the National Survey on Drug Abuse indicates that the young adult group is clearly the predominant cocaine-using group for the entire period from 1974–1982. Between 1979 and 1982 the trends for use in the past year (Annual Prevalence) for both youth (12–17) and young adults were stable or decreasing slightly. In contrast, the annual prevalence rate for older adults (age 26 and older) was increasing (Table 2).

It has been suggested that this increase in cocaine use among older adults is a cohort effect, that is, the result of the aging of the young adult population rather than the result of new use in the older population.

New Use Among Older Adults

A recent analysis examined the extent to which the increase in use of marijuana and cocaine among the age 26 and over group was a cohort effect. The change in the user population age 26 and older was modeled by the following equation:

$$Y-X = A + N-Q-D,$$

where X = users in 1979
        Y = users in 1982
        A = users in 1982, age 26 or older, who were under age 26 in 1979
        N = new users in 1982 who were 26 or older in 1979 and didn't use in 1979
        Q = users in 1979, age 26 or older, who didn't use in 1982 (quitters)
        D = users in 1979, age 26 or older, who died by 1982

(Note that Q = O for "ever used")

X and Y are known from the National Survey on Drug Abuse and A can be computed as follows:[6,7]

$$A = Y_{26} + Y_{27} + 1/2\ Y_{28},$$

where Y_i = number of users age i in 1982

By letting $d = N\text{-}Q\text{-}D$, the equation for the change in the user population between 1979 and 1982 simplifies to:

$$Y-X = A + d,$$

where   d = net change in users among 26 and older cohort in
1979

When this model was applied to marijuana data, the significant
increase in lifetime marijuana use in the National Survey between
1979 and 1982 was found to be the result of the cohort effect (Table
3). When the 23–25 year old cohort was excluded, the net change
in the number of users was not statistically significant, suggesting
little or no new use within the older adult group. However, the 23–25
year old cohort added nearly 6 million new marijuana users to the 26
and older age group.

When the model was applied to cocaine data, on the other hand,
the significant increases in the number of lifetime and annual cocaine
users were only partially explained by a cohort effect (Table 4). In
addition to the large number of people in the 23–25 year old cohort
entering the older category who were users in 1982, there was an
equally large net increase in new users within the older adult group,
indicating many new older adult cocaine users.

TABLE 2

Trends in Past Year and Past Month Use of Cocaine
by Age Category
1972-1982

| | Estimated Percent of the Population | | | | | |
	1972	1974	1976	1977	1979	1982
Age 12-17						
Used in Past Year	1.5	2.7	2.3	2.6	4.2	4.1
Used in Past Month	.6	1.0	1.0	.8	1.4	1.6
Age 18-25						
Used in Past Year	NA	8.1	7.0	10.2	19.6	18.8
Used in Past Month	NA	3.1	2.0	3.7	9.3	6.8
Age 26 and Above						
Used in Past Year	NA	*	.6	.9	2.0	3.8
Used in Past Month	NA	*	*	*	.9	1.2

*Less than 0.5%

Source: NIDA, unpublished data from the National Survey on Drug Abuse

TABLE 3

Changes in Number of Marijuana Users Age 26 and Older
Between 1979 and 1982

	Ever Used	Used in Past Year	Used in Past Month
Number in 1979 (X)	23,940,000	10,970,000	7,400,000
Number in 1982 (Y)	29,190,000	13,490,000	8,370,000
Statistical significance (H_0: Y-X = 0)	.013	NS	NS
Increase due to aging cohort (A)	5,987,000	3,100,000	1,834,000
Net change excluding cohort effect (d)	-737,000	-580,000	-864,000
Statistical significance of d (H_0: d = 0)	NS	NS	NS

TABLE 4

Changes in Number of Cocaine Users Age 26 and Older
Between 1979 and 1982

	Ever Used	Used in Past Year	Used in Past Month
Number in 1979 (X)	5,190,000	2,420,000	1,070,000
Number in 1982 (Y)	10,820,000	4,810,000	1,550,000
Statistical significance (H_0: Y-X = 0)	.001	.002	NS
Increase due to aging cohort (A)	2,577,000	1,285,000	266,000
Net change excluding cohort effect (d)	+3,053,000	+1,105,000	+214,000
Statistical significance of d (H_0: d = 0)	.002	.087	NS

Further analysis of the new cocaine users age 26 and older suggests that these new users are more likely to be unmarried, employed, college graduates, residing in a metropolitan area and in the western United States. Interestingly, income was not significantly different between the new cocaine users and all 26–50 year olds (Table 5). The frequency and recency of marijuana use were

TABLE 5

Demographic Characteristics of New Cocaine Users
Age 26 and Older
(First Use Within Past 3 Years and After Age 25)

Demographics	New Cocaine Users (n = 82)	All 26-50 Yr. Olds (n = 2102)	t-test (5% sig. level)
% White	86	79	NS
% Male	53	48	NS
% West region	38	21	S
% Metro area	95	79	S
% Not married	65	35	S
% College graduate	44	26	S
% Employed	91	76	S
% Manager or professional	61	35	S
% Income ≥ $30,000	34	31	NS

Source: NIDA, unpublished data from the National Survey on Drug Abuse, 1982

important predictors of new cocaine use but use of marijuana before age 18 was not (Table 6).

These findings suggest that: (a) cocaine users are not "naive" users in the sense that they have used illicit drugs in the past, and (b) the period of risk for cocaine use is longer than for other drugs.

The latter suggestion is consistent with research reported by Kandel which suggests that the hazard rate or risk of incidence for marijuana peaks at age 18 and declines steadily after that while that for cocaine increases steadily through the mid-20's.[8]

Similarly, O'Malley et al., have demonstrated that the prevalence of cocaine use increases with each successive year following graduation from high school (Figure 1).[9] As with Kandel's findings, other illicit drugs show little change or even show decreases in use subsequent to graduation.

Characteristics of Cocaine Users

Unlike the past when drug use, including cocaine use, was confined to selected subpopulations, today cocaine use is distributed throughout our population (Tables 7,8). While cocaine use appears to be higher among those with at least a high school diploma or who are employed, it should be noted that prevalence is relatively similar for all income groups. As previously noted, income did not differ significantly between new cocaine users and the general 26–50 year old population. Also interesting is the difference in prevalence by sex between youth and adults 18–44. While lifetime prevalence for adults reflects the male predominance in illicit drug use that has been the pattern in our society, the lifetime prevalence rates for males and females among youth are almost equal. This may reflect a slowly narrowing gap in use between males and females.

Recent Trends in Cocaine Use

Through 1983, data from the High School Senior Survey reflected trends similar to those seen in the National Household Survey (Table 9).[10] Both annual and lifetime prevalence remained relatively stable between 1979–1984. Since 1983 there have been significant increases among high school seniors in cocaine use in the past 30 days; 6.7 percent of the senior class reported current cocaine use in 1985. Increases were also noted for use in the past year and lifetime use. All three measures of prevalence represent new peak

TABLE 6

Drug Use of New Cocaine Users
Age 26 and Older
(First Use Within Past 3 Years and After Age 25)

Drug Use	New Cocaine Users (n = 82)	All 26-50 Yr. Olds Who Have Used Marijuana But Not Cocaine (n = 628)	t-test (5% sig. level)
Cocaine			
% Past month	21	0	-
% Past year	57	0	-
Marijuana			
% Past month	51	14	S
% Past year	74	29	S
% Ever	96	100	NS
% At least 100 times	53	14	S
% First use before age 18	22	21	NS

Source: NIDA, unpublished data from the National Survey on Drug Abuse, 1982

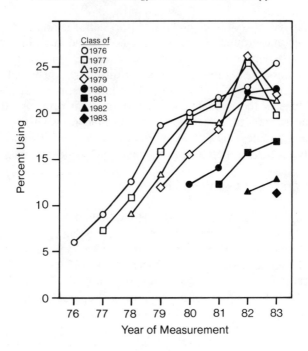

Figure 1.
Annual cocaine prevalence, classes of 1976-1983.

levels. Much of the increase in 1984 was driven by a sharp rise in current use in the northeast. In 1985, while the increase in the northeast continued, additional increases in use were noted in the western and north-central regions.

While data from the 1982 National Survey on Drug Abuse suggest that the epidemic increases in the 1970's may have abated, the current high school senior data suggests an increase from the plateau seen in the early 80's. Recent reports of increasing emergency room cases associated with cocaine, increasing deaths, and rising treatment admissions for cocaine problems also have caused many to suggest that the incidence (new use) of cocaine use may be increasing once again. Data from recent public opinion polls (Gallup, Washington Post-ABC News) do not provide evidence of any major changes in prevalence levels since 1982 (Table 10).[11] However, these surveys are not strictly comparable to the National Survey on Drug Abuse due to methodological differences. Until the results of the 1985 National

Survey on Drug Abuse are known, a valid assessment of the current trend in the general population cannot be made.

Use of Other Drugs By Cocaine Users

It seems that today some people view cocaine use as if it were a separate drug-using phenomenon. On the contrary, people who use cocaine have already experienced the use of other drugs, especially marijuana. As noted in Table 11, 98 percent of the people who have tried cocaine in their lifetime have also used marijuana and at least 93 percent used marijuana first. Furthermore, the probability of cocaine use increases with the frequency of marijuana use (Table 12). Nearly three-fourths of adults who have used marijuana 100 or

TABLE 7

Cocaine Use by Demographic and Other Characteristics

Subgroup	% Ever Used Youth 12-17	% Ever Used Adults 18-44	% Used in Past Month Youth 12-17*	% Used in Past Month Adults 18-44
Total	6.5	22.0	* N is too small to report	4.3
Sex				
Male	6.5	28.0		6.0
Female	6.4	16.3		2.7
Race				
White	6.8	23.7		4.7
Other	5.3	15.3		2.4
Region				
Northeast	8.3	25.4		6.9
North Central	3.4	17.3		3.4
South	5.7	15.8		2.2
West	10.0	34.1		5.8
Population Density				
Large Metro	9.0	25.9		5.0
Other Metro	5.4	22.5		4.5
Non-Metro	4.2	14.7		2.7

Source: NIDA, unpublished data from the National Survey on Drug Abuse, 1982

TABLE 8

Cocaine Use by Socio-economic Characteristics
Among Adults 18-44

Subgroup	% Ever Used	% Used in Past Month
Education		
High School Graduate	23.3	4.5
Not H.S. Graduate	14.6	2.7
Employment		
Employed	24.3	5.0
Not Employed	15.3	2.2
Occupation		
Not Asked	15.2	2.2
Professionals/Managers	28.4	5.9
Skilled/Retail	19.9	4.2
Other	23.8	4.7
Family Income		
Under $10,000	26.1	3.9
$10-19,999	24.3	5.6
$20-29,999	20.0	2.7
Over $30,000	20.6	4.8
Unknown	13.4	3.0

Source: NIDA, unpublished data from the National Survey on Drug Abuse, 1982

more times have tried cocaine. Past month marijuana users and frequent marijuana users are also more likely to be users of cocaine in the past month (Table 13.)

A similar pattern was found in the High School Senior Survey where 84 percent of the current cocaine users are also current marijuana users. In addition, 80 percent of current cocaine users reported having 5 or more drinks in a row at least once in the 2 weeks prior to interview and 50 percent smoke cigarettes daily.[9]

Thus, the population at risk for cocaine use has not only tried marijuana but is more likely to be current and frequent users of marijuana. This is significant in that it implies that the reported reduction in marijuana use may ultimately be reflected in a diminution of the population at risk for cocaine use.

PROGRESSION IN USE

Another issue of importance in assessing the cocaine problem is that of progression. It has been demonstrated that current and frequent marijuana users are more likely to try cocaine, but are they likely to become frequent users of cocaine? That is, will they progress to more intensive and destructive patterns of cocaine use? O'Malley

TABLE 9

Trends in Current, Annual and Lifetime Prevalence
of Cocaine Use Among High School Seniors
(Percent of Seniors in Class)
1975 - 1985

	1975	1976	1977	1978	1979	1980	1981	1982	1983	1984	1985
Current	1.9	2.0	2.9	3.9	5.7	5.2	5.8	5.0	4.9	5.8	6.7
Annual	5.6	6.0	7.2	9.0	12.0	12.3	12.4	11.5	11.4	11.6	13.1
Lifetime	9.0	9.7	10.8	12.9	15.4	15.7	16.5	16.0	16.2	16.1	17.3

Source: Johnston LD, O'Malley PM, Bachman JG. Use of licit and illicit
drugs by America's high school students, 1975-1984. DHHS Pub. No.
(ADM) 85-1394. Washington, D.C.: U.S. Govt. Print. Off., 1985.
pp. 34-36, and unpublished data from the 1985 High School Senior
Survey.

TABLE 10

Current, Annual and Lifetime Prevalence
of Cocaine Use by Age
U.S. Males, 1984

	% Ever Used	% Used in Past Year	% Used in Past Month
Total Males (age 18+)	21.1	7.6	3.8
18-25 yrs	37	20	10
26-34	31	13	7
35+	13	2	1

Source: Unpublished data from the Gallup Poll, 1984

TABLE 11

Sequence of Use of Marijuana Among Lifetime Cocaine Users
(Persons who have used cocaine at least once)

	Percent Distribution
Never used marijuana	2
Used cocaine, then later marijuana	1
First used cocaine and marijuana at same age	4
Used marijuana, then later cocaine	93

Source: NIDA, unpublished data from the National Survey on Drug Abuse, 1982

TABLE 12

Lifetime Cocaine Use Among Adults 18 Years and Older
According to Recency and Frequency of Marijuana Use

Recency of Marijuana Use	% Ever Used Cocaine	% Never Used Cocaine
Never used marijuana	0.3	99.7
Used marijuana, but ≤10 times and not past month	11.2	88.8
Used marijuana >10 times, but not past month	44.2	55.8
Used marijuana in past month	68.4	31.6
Frequency of Marijuana Use in Lifetime		
Never	0.3	99.7
1-2	1.8	98.2
3-10	21.8	78.2
11-99	40.8	59.2
100+	74.0	26.0

Source: NIDA, unpublished data from the National Survey on Drug Abuse, 1982

et al., have analyzed data from the followup of high school seniors using an index based on frequency of use (Table 14). The analysis includes the graduation year, a first followup 1–2 years later, and a second followup 3 to 4 years past graduation. For the base year measurement, only 1.2 percent of the responding population had used cocaine 10 or more times during the previous year, while at the second followup in a population now aged 21–22, 4.7 percent of the population had used 10 or more times in the previous year. It is interesting to note the transition between levels of use. Thus, while it seems that there is some progression, progression is not inevitable.[9] Similar findings have also been noted by Siegel and Chitwood.[12,13]

Use in Combination With Other Drugs

Consistent with clinical studies, data from the Gallup Poll indicate that cocaine users not only use other drugs, but also that they often use these drugs in combination with cocaine (Table 15).

The pharmacological nature of the interactions of many of substances commonly used in combination with cocaine is yet to be adequately researched. People who use cocaine in combination with other drugs or are multiple drug users have been found to have more psychopathology, increased risk of a variety of medical conditions, and more severe withdrawal symptoms.[14–16] Many of these people

TABLE 13

Cocaine Use in the Past Month Among Adults
18 Years and Older According to Recency
and Frequency of Marijuana Use

Recency of Marijuana Use	% Used Cocaine in Past Month	% Not Using Cocaine in Past Month
Never used marijuana	0.0	100.0
Used marijuana, but ≤10 times and not past month	1.0	99.0
Used marijuana >10 times, but not past month	7.5	92.5
Used marijuana in past month	15.0	85.0
Frequency of Marijuana Use in Lifetime		
Never	0.0	100.0
1-2	0.4	99.6
3-10	2.4	97.6
11-99	9.4	90.6
100+	14.1	85.9

Source: NIDA, unpublished data from the National Survey on Drug Abuse, 1982

TABLE 14

Longitudinal Patterns of Annual Use of Cocaine
Classes of 1976-1980

Base-Year Use	First Followup Use	Second Followup Use
	84.12% (None)	75.39% (None) 7.59% (<Ten) 1.14% (Ten+)
92.18% (None)	6.85% (<Ten)	2.33% (None) 3.46% (<Ten) 1.06% (Ten+)
	1.23% (Ten+)	0.20% (None) 0.55% (<Ten) 0.48% (Ten+)
	2.14% (None)	1.25% (None) 0.71% (<Ten) 0.18% (Ten+)
6.63% (<Ten)	3.35% (<Ten)	0.81% (None) 1.79% (<Ten) 0.75% (Ten+)
	1.13% (Ten+)	0.09% (None) 0.38% (<Ten) 0.67% (Ten+)
	0.28% (None)	0.20% (None) 0.08% (<Ten) 0.01% (Ten+)
1.20% (Ten+)	0.38% (<Ten)	0.05% (None) 0.21% (<Ten) 0.13% (Ten+)
	0.52% (Ten+)	0.03% (None) 0.22% (<Ten) 0.27% (Ten+)

Notes: Data are based on approximately 7,000 respondents who participated in two followups.

Entries sum up to 100% within each column.

Source: See Reference No. 9

are, in fact, dually addicted to both cocaine and alcohol and require more complex treatment regimens.

Health Consequences

A variety of adverse physical and psychological effects associated with cocaine have been reported in clinical and laboratory

Adams et al.   *63*

studies. The nature and severity of the effects of cocaine use on health and functioning are determined by such factors as purity, dose, duration of use, route of administration, and the user's prior medical history.

The dangers involved with cocaine use include both acute and chronic use consequences affecting the cardiovascular, respiratory, and central nervous systems. Acute cocaine toxicity, similar to that for amphetamines, is characterized by nervousness, dizziness, blurred vision, and tremors, and could eventuate in convulsions, cardiac arrhythmias and respiratory arrest.[17] In fatal cases of cocaine poisoning, the rapid onset of symptoms and progression to the most severe phase of toxicity may occur within 1–2 minutes.[18] Chronic toxicity occurs with continued use of high doses of cocaine. Chronic use is also associated with ulceration and perforation of the nasal septum, weight loss, insomnia, anxiety, paranoia, formication, hallucinations, and depression.[19–24]

Physical problems have been associated with route of administration.[12,13] Intranasal users ("snorters") are more likely to have sinusitis, rhinitis, or an ulcerated or perforated nasal septum and upper respiratory infections.[18] Intravenous users, in contrast, have significantly more hepatitis, abscesses or other skin infections; these consequences as well as the incidence of AIDS among cocaine users[25] are usually attributed to the use of nonsterile needles. Cocaine freebase users, that is, those who smoke cocaine, are more

TABLE 15

Percent of Last Year Cocaine Users Combining
Other Drugs With Cocaine
By Age Group and Drug Combinations
U.S. Males, 1984

	Total Males Age 18+	18-25 yrs.	26-34 yrs.	35+
Cocaine + Alcohol	49%	34%	60%	64%
Cocaine + Marijuana	35%	27%	50%	22%
Cocaine + Amphetamines	8%	10%	9%	-
Cocaine + Tranquilizers	5%	9%	3%	-
Cocaine + Opiates	4%	4%	4%	-

Source: Unpublished data from the Gallup Poll, 1984

likely to have pulmonary dysfunctioning,[24] bronchitis, voice loss, chest pains, and seizures.[12,18]

Several researchers have demonstrated that intravenous use and the smoking of freebase lead to more rapid absorption and shorter duration of action than intranasal use.[26-28] It has also been suggested that smoking freebase and intravenous use lead to continuous consumption and drug-seeking behavior.[26] Data from treatment admissions do in fact reflect a greater likelihood of daily use by intravenous and freebase users than by intranasal users.[29] In addition, these routes of administration are increasingly reported in treatment and emergency room admissions. However, intranasal use is still the primary route reported at admission to treatment. In addition, it has been suggested that the dangers of intranasal use have been underestimated.[30] Severe psychological distress has been reported by cocaine abusers regardless of the usual route of administration.[31,32]

Cocaine Related Emergencies

Data on adverse health consequences as reflected by hospital emergency room visits and medical examiner cases are collected by NIDA through the Drug Abuse Warning Network (DAWN). While cocaine mentions in DAWN have been increasing for several years, there has been a particularly dramatic rise in cocaine mentions from emergency rooms since the first quarter of 1983 (Figure 2).[33]

Recently, we have initiated a special study of cocaine trends using a 9-year panel of consistently reporting hospitals from DAWN. The data reflect more than a 7-fold increase in the rate of emergency room visits for cocaine related problems per 100,000 emergency visits (10.4 to 75.4). While the rate has been greater for hospitals located in the center cities, parallel increases have been seen also in hospitals located in areas surrounding the center city. Virtually all cities have experienced this increase in cocaine-related cases (Table 15).

As has been mentioned previously, cocaine users often use other drugs. More than two-thirds of the cocaine related emergency room episodes are in combination with other drugs. Cocaine is mentioned in 3 of the top 10 combinations of drugs reported in DAWN emergency rooms from January to November 1984. The combination of heroin and cocaine, known as a "speedball," was the second most frequently mentioned combination in DAWN.

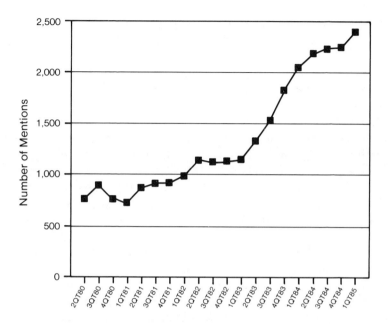

Figure 2.
Cocaine mentions in DAWN emergency rooms by quarter,
2nd quarter 1980—1st quarter 1985

Cocaine Treatment Admissions

Data on admissions to drug abuse treatment were collected through the Client Oriented Data Acquisition Process (CODAP) which was a national reporting system of primarily publicly-funded programs through 1981. Since 1981, treatment data have been collected on a voluntary basis. Currently, there are approximately 15 States that report treatment data to NIDA. The data reflect continuing increases in both primary and secondary cocaine admissions to treatment programs reporting to NIDA. In 1977, primary cocaine admissions accounted for 1.8 percent of all admissions to CODAP while in 1981 they accounted for 5.8 percent. If secondary cocaine admissions are included, the increase for overall cocaine mentions in CODAP was from 10 percent in 1977 to 17 percent in 1981.

Although the treatment data for 1983 and 1984 are no longer

directly comparable to previous data because they reflect only 15 to 20 States, the provisional data currently available do provide an interesting look at a large number of treatment admissions. In 1983, primary cocaine problems accounted for 7.3 percent of all admissions and secondary cocaine problems for 10.5 percent. For the first 6 months of 1984, however, primary cocaine admissions represented 13.9 percent of all admissions and secondary cocaine admissions represented an additional 14.9 percent. Thus, more than one-fourth (28.7%) of the treatment clients now reported to NIDA have a problem with cocaine.

In the current treatment population the median age of first use of cocaine is 20. This reflects a trend toward older ages of first use as noted previously.[29] In 1977, for example, 40 percent of primary cocaine admissions in treatment had begun use by age 17 or younger; by 1981 the percentage had been reduced to 32 percent. Recent treatment data indicate that this trend may be continuing with only 26 percent of the clients for whom data are now available having begun cocaine use before their 18th birthday. Among the primary cocaine admissions, approximately two-thirds of the individuals over 18 have at least a high school diploma and almost 44 percent are employed either full or part-time. Approximately 31 percent of the primary cocaine admissions in 1984 were 30 years of age or older. The age distribution for secondary cocaine admissions, which reflect the use of speedballing, is even older with approximately 49 percent being age 30 or older (Table 16).

While snorting or inhalation continues to be the predominant mode of administration representing 57 percent of recent treatment admissions, freebasing or smoking cocaine increased substantially from less than 1 percent in 1977 to 4.7 percent in 1981 and is now reported, based on the 1984 data, by 16 percent of primary cocaine clients. Injection as a route of administration is reported by almost 25 percent of the primary cocaine admissions. These intravenous cocaine users do not include the majority of the speedballing population who generally report cocaine as their secondary problem (Table 17).

Consistent with both survey and DAWN data, cocaine treatment clients often use other drugs. Eighty-one percent of primary cocaine admissions in 1984 also reported problems with other drugs, particularly heroin, marijuana, and alcohol.

TABLE 16

Rates of Cocaine Mentions Per 100,000 Emergency Room Visits,
by Center City for Selected Cities

City	July 1975-June 1976	July 1979-June 1980	July 1983-June 1984
Atlanta	3.9	13.9	15.0
Baltimore	1.6	7.3	3.1
Boston	7.0	19.9	45.5
Buffalo	1.5	7.5	19.7
Chicago	3.7	17.9	50.9
Cleveland	1.6	11.6	29.9
Dallas	1.6	3.5	15.2
Denver	4.5	21.1	50.6
Detroit	12.0	23.2	119.5
Indianapolis	3.6	7.6	14.7
Kansas City	4.3	7.2	24.2
Los Angeles	9.5	12.9	119.7
Miami	92.6	218.7	306.2
Minneapolis	5.9	11.3	27.2
New Orleans	1.2	21.8	184.8
New York	22.0	41.6	144.1
Oklahoma City	0.0	3.9	23.4
Philadelphia	2.6	9.6	40.2
Phoenix	7.7	26.1	34.9
St. Louis	0.0	8.4	0.0
San Antonio	0.0	1.9	7.7
San Diego	1.6	4.5	13.8
San Francisco	34.5	40.9	215.0
Seattle	16.4	26.9	71.2
Washington, D.C.	3.8	11.0	46.6
Total DAWN System	10.4	25.5	75.4

Data are based on a 9-year consistent reporting panel.

Source: NIDA, unpublished data from the Drug Abuse Warning Network

TABLE 17

Percent Distribution
Route of Administration by Age of Admission
for Primary Cocaine Admissions
(Jan-Jun 1984)

Route of Administration	10-19	20-24	25-29	Age 30-34	35-39	40+	Total
Oral	2.1	1.1	1.1	2.1	1.9	2.1	1.5
Smoking	9.1	15.9	15.6	16.5	18.7	19.5	15.7
Snorting	76.5	61.0	54.6	49.9	49.5	55.2	57.1
Injection	12.2	21.5	28.1	31.2	29.7	21.6	24.7
Total N	773	2554	2796	1647	701	375	8846
Primary Admissions %	8.7	28.9	31.6	18.6	7.9	4.2	100
Secondary Admissions N	643	1890	2980	2878	1435	881	10707
%	6.1	17.6	27.8	26.9	13.4	8.2	100

Source: NIDA, unpublished treatment data

SUMMARY

Illicit drug use spread throughout the younger population in the 1960's. This increase in use did not include cocaine to a great extent. However, epidemic increases in the incidence of cocaine use occurred in the country in the mid to late 1970's. Between 1979 and 1982, prevalence seems to have leveled off for young people, but use among adults age 26 and older increased. More recent data from the High School Senior Survey show current increases in prevalence for this youthful population. Data from public opinion polls, while not directly comparable to the National Survey on Drug Use, do not provide evidence of further increases in the general adult population. Until the results of the 1985 National Survey on Drug Abuse are available, an accurate comparable assessment of trends in cocaine prevalence in the general population since 1982 cannot be made.

Data from emergency rooms and from treatment admissions show increases since 1982. These increases may reflect a pattern of more frequent use and more dangerous routes of administration, such as injection and freebasing, by a subset of the cocaine-using population. As indicated in survey data, DAWN data and treatment data, the cocaine-using population is a multi-drug-using population, suggesting that cocaine abuse may not be a singular syndrome. The apparent heterogeneity of cocaine users, in terms of demographic, socioeconomic, cultural, and environmental characteristics, combined with differing drug use patterns and combinations, suggests that a number of different treatment settings and approaches may be required to deal with the cocaine problem.

REFERENCES

1. Adams EH. The epidemiology of cocaine abuse. Presented at the Regent Progress Symposium, Cocaine Abuse: Recognition and Treatment, Fair Oaks Hospital, Summit, New Jersey, May 8, 1982.
2. National Commission on Marihuana and Drug Abuse. Drug use in America: Problem in perspective. Second report of the National Commission on Marihuana and Drug Abuse. Washington, D.C.: National Institute on Drug Abuse, March 1973.
3. Strategy Council on Drug Abuse. Federal strategy for drug abuse and drug traffic prevention 1973. Washington, D.C.: Supt. of Docs., U.S. Govt. Print. Off., 1973.
4. Adams EH, Durell J. Cocaine: A growing public health problem. In: Grabowski J, ed. Cocaine: Pharmacology, effects, and treatment of abuse. (NIDA Research Monograph #50, DHHS Pub. No. (ADM) 84–1326.) Washington, D.C.: Supt. of Docs., U.S. Govt. Print. Off., 1984. pp. 9–14.
5. Blanken AJ, Adams EH, Durell J. Drug abuse: Implications and current trends. Psychiatric Medicine, in press.
6. National Institute on Drug Abuse. Population Projections, Based on the National Survey on Drug Abuse, 1979. Washington, D.C., U.S. Govt. Print. Off., GPO 883–317, 1981.
7. National Institute on Drug Abuse. Population projections, based on the National Survey on Drug Abuse, 1982. DHHS Pub. No. (ADM) 83–1303. Washington, D.C.: Supt. of Docs., U.S. Govt. Print. Off., 1983.
8. Kandel DB, Murphy D, Karus D. Cocaine use in young adulthood: Patterns of use and psychosocial correlates. In: Kozel NJ, Adams EH, eds. Cocaine use in America: Epidemiologic and clinical perspectives. (NIDA Research Monograph #61, DHHS Pub. No. (ADM) 85–1414.) Washington, D.C.: Supt. of Docs., U.S. Govt. Print. Off., 1985.
9. O'Malley PM, Johnston LD, Bachman JG. Cocaine use among American adolescents and young adults. In: Kozel NJ, Adams EH, eds. Cocaine use in America: Epidemiologic and clinical perspectives. (NIDA Research Monograph #61, DHHS Pub. No. (ADM) 85–1414.) Washington, D.C.: U.S. Govt. Print. Off., 1985.
10. Johnston LD, O'Malley PM, Bachman JG, Use of licit and illicit drugs by America's high school students, 1975–1984. DHHS Pub. No. (ADM) 85–1394. Washington, D.C.: U.S. Govt. Print. Off., 1985.
11. Sussman B. Drug use tops '60s level, Washington Post, June 12, 1985.
12. Siegel RK. New patterns of cocaine use: Changing doses and routes. In: Kozel NJ, Adams EH, eds. Cocaine use in America: Epidemiologic and clinical perspectives. (NIDA Research Monograph #61, DHHS Pub. No. (ADM) 85–1414.) Washington, D.C.: U.S. Govt. Print. Off., 1985.
13. Chitwood DD. Patterns and consequences of cocaine use. In: Kozel NJ, Adams EH, eds. Cocaine use in America: Epidemiologic and clinical perspectives. (NIDA Research

Monograph #61, DHHS Pub. No. (ADM) 85–1414.) Washington, D.C.: U.S. Govt. Print. Off., 1985.

14. Kaufman E. The abuse of multiple drugs: (1) Definition, classification, and extent of problems. Am J Drug Alcohol Abuse 1976; 3(2):279–292.

15. Schuster CR, Fischman MW. Characteristics of humans volunteering for a cocaine research project. In: Kozel NJ, Adams EH, eds. Cocaine use in America: Epidemiologic and clinical perspectives. (NIDA Research Monograph #61, DHHS Pub. No. (ADM) 85–1414.) Washington, D.C.: U.S. Govt. Print. Off., 1985.

16. Wesson DR, Smith DE. Cocaine: Treatment perspectives. In: Kozel NJ, Adams EH, eds. Cocaine use in America: Epidemiologic and clinical perspectives. (NIDA Research Monograph #61, DHHS Pub. No. (ADM) 85–1414.) Washington, D.C.: U.S. Govt. Print. Off., 1985.

17. Schachne JS, Roberts BH, Thompson PD. Coronary artery spasm and myocardial infarction associated with cocaine use. N Engl J Med 1984; 310(25):1665–1666.

18. Gay GR. Clinical management of acute and chronic cocaine poisoning. Annals Emergency Med 1982; 11:562–572.

19. Young D, Glauber JJ. Electrocardiographic changes resulting from acute cocaine intoxication. Am Heart J 1947; 34:272–279.

20. Gay GR, Inaba DS, Sheppard CW, Newmeyer, JA. Cocaine: History, epidemiology, human pharmacology and treatment. A perspective on a new debut for an old girl. Clin Toxicol 1975; 8(2):149–178.

21. Jonsson S, O'Meara M, Young JB. Acute cocaine poisoning. Importance of treating seizures and acidosis. Am J Med 1983; 75(6)1061–1064.

22. Lichtenfeld PJ, Rubin DB, Feldman RS. Subarachnoid hemorrhage precipitated by cocaine snorting. Arch Neurol 1984; 41(2):223–224.

23. Nanji AA, Filipenko JD. Asystoll and ventricular fibrillation associated with cocaine intoxication. Chest 1984; 85(1):132–133.

24. Weiss RD, Goldenheim PD, Mirin SM, Hales CA, Mendelson JH. Pulmonary dysfunction in cocaine smokers. Am J Psychiatry 1982; 138(8): 1110–1112.

25. Marmor M, Des Jarlais DC, Friedman SR, Lyden M, El-Sadr W. The epidemic of acquired immunodeficiency syndrome (AIDS) and suggestions for the control in drug abusers. J Substance Abuse Treatment 1984; 1:237–247.

26. Van Dyke C, Byck R. Cocaine. Scientific American 1982; 246:128–141.

27. Fischman MW. The behavioral pharmacology of cocaine in humans. In: Grabowski J, ed. Cocaine: Pharmacology, effects, and treatment of abuse. (NIDA Research Monograph #50, DHHS Pub. No. (ADM) 84–1326.) Washington, D.C.: Supt. of Docs., U.S. Govt. Print. Off., 1984. pp. 72–91.

28. Jones RT. The pharmacology of cocaine. In: Grabowski J, ed. Cocaine: Pharmacology, effects, and treatment of abuse. (NIDA Research Monograph #50, DHHS Pub. No. (ADM) 84–1326.) Washington, D.C.: Supt. of Docs., U.S. Govt. Print. Off., 1984. pp. 34–53.

29. Adams EH. Abuse/availability trends of cocaine in the United States. Drug surveillance reports, Vol. 1, No. 2, 1982. Division of Epidemiology and Statistical Analysis, National Institute on Drug Abuse. Rockville, MD: The Institute, 1982.

30. Gawin FH, Kleber HD. Cocaine use in a treatment population: Patterns and diagnostic distinctions. In: Kozel NJ, Adams EH, eds. Cocaine use in America: Epidemiologic and clinical perspectives. (NIDA Research Monograph #61, DHHS Pub. No. (ADM) 85–1414.) Washington, D.C.: U.S. Govt. Print. Off., 1985.

31. Helfrich AA, Crowley TJ, Atkinson CA. A clinical profile of 136 cocaine abusers. In: Problems of drug dependence, 1982. (NIDA Research Monograph 43. DHHS Pub. No. (ADM) 83–1264.) Washington, D.C.: Supt. of Docs., U.S. Govt. Print. Off., 1983.

32. Gold MS, Washton AM, Dackis CA: Cocaine abuse: Neurochemistry, phenomenol-

ogy, and treatment. In: Kozel NJ, Adams EH, eds. Cocaine use in America: Epidemiologic and clinical perspectives. (NIDA Research Monograph #61, DHHS Pub. No. (ADM) 85–1414.) Washington, D.C.: U.S. Govt. Print. Off., 1985.

33. Adams EH, Gfroerer JC, Blanken AJ. Prevalence, patterns and consequences of cocaine use. In: Brink CH, ed. Cocaine: A symposium. Madison: Wisconsin Institute of Drug Abuse, 1985. pp. 37–42.

Cocaine Use
Among Young Adults

Michael D. Newcomb, PhD
P. M. Bentler, PhD

ABSTRACT. The use of cocaine has become quite prevalent among many segments of society, with increasing public concern and personal difficulties resulting from it. This study examines a large group of young adults to determine how cocaine users differ from nonusers. Fully one-third of the sample had used cocaine in the past six months, with about 5% reporting weekly or more use. Numerous important differences were found between users and nonusers in regard to sociodemographic characteristics, use of other licit and illicit drugs, deviant attitudes and behavior, social context of use, physical health, mental health, and life satisfaction. Differences increased with greater involvement with the drug, to the point where cocaine abusers were strikingly different than nonusers. The largest distinctions were noted in regard to cocaine users having more difficulty in the successful acquisition of adult role responsibilities, greater use of other drugs, engaging in more deviant behaviors, and immersion in a social context conducive to use. Smaller but noteworthy differences revealed that cocaine users had poor physical and emotional health statuses and lowered life satisfaction, compared to nonusers. Finally, several personality traits, and in particular a lack of law abidance, predicted a significant increase in cocaine use from adolescence to young adulthood.

Although marijuana is currently the most widely used illicit drug substance, nonmedical, self-administered use of cocaine has increased dramatically during the 1970s.[1] For instance, one study found that about 5% of college students used cocaine in 1969

Michael D. Newcomb and P. M. Bentler are affiliated with the University of California, Los Angeles, CA. This research was partially supported by grants DA01070 and DA00017 from the National Institute on Drug Abuse. The assistance of Julie Speckart and Sandy Yu is gratefully acknowledged. Address correspondence and reprint request to: Dr. Michael D. Newcomb, Department of Psychology, University of California, Los Angeles, CA 90024.

compared to 30% in 1978.[2] More recently, there appears to be a
leveling trend in the 1980s.[3] However, the most recent evidence
indicates that this leveling trend is apparent only in certain geo-
graphical locations in the U.S., and that, in fact, increases in
cocaine use are continuing in the northeast portions of the country.[4]
In 1984, 16% of high school seniors reported having used cocaine
at least once, and 6% reported use during the past month.[4] As part
of a longitudinal study of adolescents, 4% of the sample reported
cocaine use as seventh through ninth graders in 1976, which
increased to 11% in 1979, and 20% in 1980.[5] Rates of use have
been reported even higher for young adult populations, ranging over
30%.[6-7]

Cocaine abuse is prevalent among all segments of society. There
is accumulating evidence of increased cocaine precipitated hospital
admissions, toxic psychoses, severe psychological dependencies,
and deaths.[8-10] Numerous professional and self-help groups, such as
Cocaine Anonymous, have emerged to meet the increasing personal
and social problems resulting from cocaine abuse. Stories abound
about those who have created financial ruin and personal tragedies
of damaged or destroyed relationships with lovers, friends, and
family while pursuing the alluring appeal of scoring the next gram
or snorting the next line.

Typical acute reactions to cocaine use include increased heart
rate, elevated blood pressure, lowered skin temperature, mild
tremors, euphoric mood, relief of fatigue and boredom, increased
body temperature, and slightly dilated pupils.[11] Although earlier
research found inconclusive results regarding the addictive potential
of cocaine,[12] more recent findings indicate that repeated cocaine use
appears to have both physically and psychologically addictive
qualities.[13-14] The most addictive component of cocaine is its
euphoric psychological effect. The drug produces an extremely
pleasurable and ecstatic mood, and thus is quite reinforcing.[15-16]
When the euphoria fades—after a very short period of time because
it is rapidly metabolized—there is typically a rebound dysphoria or
depression, often leading to a frantic search for more cocaine to
prevent such discomfort and to reinstate the high.[17]

Although there have been numerous studies examining the
physiological mechanisms involved in cocaine use, very few studies
have addressed the psychological concomitants of use and the type
of person who becomes involved with cocaine. Some researchers

have reported that cocaine use is associated with the use of licit and other illicit drugs. For instance, Mills and Noyes[18] found that cocaine was associated with marijuana use among a group of adolescents. Newcomb and Bentler[5] extended these findings by showing that those who used cocaine are significantly more likely to use many other substances including cigarettes, all types of alcohol, cannabis, over-the-counter drugs, as well as virtually all other types of hard drugs (e.g., barbiturates, LSD, heroin, and PCP). Similar findings have been reported for a sample of adult recreational cocaine users.[19]

Numerous types of psychopathology have been noted as antecedents and consequences of cocaine use. At one time, Freud touted the benefits of cocaine as a remarkable curative agent for many physical and emotional problems including depression, addiction to alcohol and morphine, and indigestion.[20] Needless to say, subsequent research has failed to corroborate these earlier expectations.[21] Over a one-year period during adolescence of a normal sample, Newcomb and Bentler found only one psychopathological antecedent and no significant consequences to cocaine use. They found that earlier depression led to increased cocaine use in the future. On the other hand, reports of toxic reactions to cocaine and cocaine induced psychosis among older, more committed cocaine users have appeared in the literature.[22-23] These accounts are based upon acute periods of intoxication, and do not determine whether more general emotional pathology is associated with cocaine use.

In this study, young adult cocaine users are compared to nonusers in regard to a variety of important life qualities both physical and emotional. Seven broad areas are considered including sociodemographic characteristics (level of assumed role responsibility), use of other psychoactive drugs, deviant attitudes and behavior, social context, physical and mental health status, and life satisfaction. Results from the literature discussed above and that related to other illicit drugs such as marijuana,[24] leads one to suspect that cocaine users may display less role responsibility, more use of other drugs, more deviant attitudes and behavior, immersion in a social context conducive to cocaine use, poorer physical and emotional health, and lowered life satisfaction. These expectations are explored in this study. Finally, several personality, psychological functioning, and social support measures are used to predict changes in cocaine use over a four-year period.

METHOD

Data were collected from 739 young adults (ages 19 to 24 years old) as part of an eight-year (fifth assessment point) longitudinal study of adolescent development and drug use.[25] The study originally began with 1,634 students in the seventh, eighth, and ninth grades, at 11 Los Angeles County schools. This study uses data from the young adult follow-up, where 45% of the original sample provided data. Attrition effects across the eight-year period are discussed elsewhere.[26]

There was a 27% attrition rate between the 1980 assessment, when subjects were in high school, and the 1984 data collection when all subjects were young adults. This subject loss was not primarily due to voluntary withdrawal from the study (less than 5% actually refused to continue). The loss of subjects was largely the result of the difficulty and frequent inability to recontact all subjects during this very mobile and change-laden period in life. In fact, many participants had to be traced to places throughout the country and all over the world. Each subject was paid $12.50 to complete the follow-up questionnaire.

Seventy percent of the sample were women and 30% were men. Current age ranged from 19 to 24 years old, with a mean of 21.5. About 32% of the sample were from minority backgrounds (Black, Hispanic, and Asian), 92% were high school graduates, average income was between $5,000 and $15,000, and 20% of the women already have had a child (only 2% of the men reported being fathers). The most frequent current life pursuit was full-time employment, followed by attending a university, and then junior college. The most typical living arrangement was staying with parents. Men seemed more likely to live with roommates and less likely to be married, than women.

In the first year of the study 64% of the sample were female and 36% were males, whereas in high school 68% were female and 32% were males. This indicates that the differential representation by sex in the young adult sample was also evident in the original sample and was not solely a result of differential attrition. The sex difference in the initial sample was due to more girls than boys being willing to participate in the study.

A series of analyses were run to determine whether the attrition in sample size from 1980 to 1984 (high school to young adulthood) was due to any systematic influence. Those who were able to be

located and provided completed questionnaires in 1984 were compared with those who were not assessed in 1984 in terms of data
obtained in 1980. These groups were contrasted in terms of 26
different drug substances and 23 personality traits from the 1980
data set. Using the Bonferroni procedure to adjust for multiple
simultaneous comparisons, not one of these 49 variables was able to
significantly differentiate the current sample from those lost at the
.05 level of significance. The average (absolute) point biserial
correlation for these 49 tests was .03, whereas the average squared
correlation was .002. The largest difference accounted for only 1%
of the variance between groups and was not significant when using
the Bonferroni method to correct for capitalizing on chance.

These analyses indicate that very little of the attrition rate
between 1980 and 1984 was due to self selection based on drug use
or personality traits. To tease out any remaining differences, a
step-wise multiple regression analysis was run using the 49 1980
drug use and personality variables as the predictor pool and
retention in 1984 as the criterion variable. Using this procedure, five
variables were chosen to differentiate the groups. Although significant, this equation choosing all of the best predictors, was only able
to account for less than 3% of the variance between groups. These
extensive analyses indicate that the loss of subjects between 1980
and 1984 was not largely due to systematic self selection or other
influences based on personality or drug use.

RESULTS

General Patterns of Use

All participants reported their frequency of cocaine use during the
past six months. Responses were given on a seven-point anchored
rating scale that ranged from never (0) to more than once per day
(6). For the men, 37% reported using cocaine at least once during
the past six months, whereas 32% of the women reported cocaine
use. When these percentages were compared statistically they were
not significantly different ($\chi^2 = 1.51$ns) indicating that one sex is
not more likely nor less likely to use cocaine than the other. The
actual frequency of use among those reporting use was also not
significantly different between men and women.

Of the men, 26% reported using cocaine a few times during the past six months, 6% reported monthly use, and 5% reported weekly or more use. For the women, 21% reported using cocaine a few times, 8% reported monthly use, and 4% reported weekly or more use.

Comparison of Users and Nonusers

A series of analyses were conducted to determine whether those who use cocaine are different from those who do not use cocaine. Users were defined as those who reported any use of cocaine during the past six months, whereas nonusers reported no use of cocaine for the same period of time. It is possible that some respondents who are classified as nonusers may have in fact used cocaine prior to the six month period. However for purposes of this paper they are considered nonusers.

Users and nonusers of cocaine were compared on seven classes of variables including sociodemographic characteristics, use of other drugs, deviant attitudes and behavior, social context of use, physical health status, mental health status, and life satisfaction. Chi-square difference in proportion tests were used to compare the groups, although only the level of significance is reported for ease of presentation. Results of these analyses are presented below in regard to each of the seven groupings of variables.

Sociodemographic Characteristics

Cocaine users (those reporting any use during the past six months) were compared to nonusers on a variety of socio-demographic variables. Results are presented in Table 1 separately by sex.

When compared to nonusers, male cocaine users were significantly more likely to have dropped out of high school before graduating, cohabited, collected unemployment, collected welfare, been fired from a job, been divorced, not attended college, not desired a college degree, and had a full-time job. Compared to nonusers, women cocaine users had more often dropped out of high school, cohabited, been fired from a job, divorced, been currently cohabiting, employed full-time, not attended college, not desired a college degree, and gone out recreationally at least one time per week. These patterns seem to be quite similar for men and women.

Additionally, level of cocaine use was compared among the four

Table 1

Sociodemographic Characteristics of Cocaine Users

	----------------Cocaine Use----------------			
	--------Men--------		--------Women-------	
	Nonuser %	User %	Nonuser %	User %
Characteristic	(N = 139)	(N = 82)	(N = 350)	(N = 168)
Is a parent	5	9	21	20
High school dropout	4	13**	6	11*
Worked ≥ 9/mo past year	63	61	50	49
Ever cohabit	21	51***	26	54***
Collected unemployment	6	18***	11	14
Collected welfare	0	2*	8	8
Collected foodstamps	1	1	4	5
Fired from job	16	26*	11	21***
Divorced	1	4*	3	6*
Earned more than $15,000	40	40	26	30
Live with spouse	11	6	25	20
Live with partner	9	15	10	17**
Desire college degree or more	70	48***	54	41***
Attended college	41	21***	35	22***
Had full time job	54	72**	54	70***
Go out at least 1x/week	63	59	60	68*

* p ≤ .05; ** p ≤ .01; *** p ≤ .001.

ethnic groups represented in the sample. A significant one-way ANOVA indicated that there were different levels of cocaine use between Blacks, Hispanics, Whites, and Asians (F = 9.79, p ≤ .001). Whites and Hispanics reported greater use of cocaine than Blacks or Asians. There were no significant differences between Whites and Hispanics, nor between Blacks and Asians.

Use of Other Drug Substances

Cocaine users were compared with nonusers in regard to whether or not they had used a variety of licit and other illicit drugs during the past six months. Results for these comparisons are presented in Table 2 for men and women.

For both men and women, cocaine users were more likely to use cigarettes, alcohol (beer, wine, or liquor), cannabis (marijuana or hashish), over-the-counter drugs (for sleep, stimulation, coughs, or colds), hypnotics (minor tranquilizers, sedatives, or barbiturates),

Table 2

Use of Other Psychoactive Drugs by Cocaine Users

Ever use past 6 months	----------------Cocaine Use----------------			
	--------Men--------		--------Women-------	
	Nonuser % (N = 139)	User % (N = 82)	Nonuser % (N = 350)	User % (N = 168)
Cigarettes	24	67***	26	65***
Alcohol	87	99***	85	99***
Cannabis	16	82***	26	80***
Over-the-counter drugs	58	72*	67	79**
Hypnotics	0	13***	1	11***
Stimulants	3	44***	4	47***
Psychedelics	1	35***	1	18***
Inhalants	2	9*	1	5***
Narcotics	1	12***	2	11***
PCP	0	4*	1	4***

* p ≤ .05; ** p ≤ .01; *** p ≤ .001.

stimulants (amphetamines or other uppers), psychedelics (LSD, mushrooms, etc.), inhalants (amyl nitrate, glue, etc.), narcotics (heroin, codeine, etc.), and PCP than those reporting no use of cocaine. In many instances, these differences are quite dramatic. For example, 82% of male cocaine users also used cannabis compared to 16% of nonusers of cocaine. Similarly large differences were apparent on cigarettes, stimulants, and psychedelics. Cocaine users were clearly more amenable to trying a variety of other drugs compared to those not using cocaine.

Deviant Attitudes and Behavior

All respondents were asked a variety of questions to determine their degree of socially conforming behavior and attitudes. Cocaine users were compared with nonusers on each of these measures and the results are presented in Table 3 separately for men and women.

Both men and women who reported using cocaine were also significantly less law abidant, more liberal, more likely to have been arrested for a drug crime (e.g., driving while intoxicated, dealing), more likely to have sold cocaine, more often used cocaine at work or school, thought that using cocaine was a good idea, and reported having had trouble with the law, alcohol, and drugs, than nonusers of cocaine. Men cocaine users also had more arrests for crimes other than drug offenses than male nonusers, whereas women cocaine users were less religious and more often involved in drug related accidents than female nonusers. Clearly, cocaine users reported more deviant attitudes and behavior than nonusers.

Social Context

The social context of cocaine use and perceived acceptability of use by others were compared between users and nonusers. Results of these analyses are presented in Table 4.

Cocaine users compared to nonusers were more likely to report peer approval for using cocaine, having read drug magazines and drug paraphenalia advertisements, and found cocaine easy to acquire. On the other hand, users were not less likely to think they would get caught or punished than nonusers. These results were apparent for men and women. Women who used cocaine reported greater perceived community approval of cocaine use.

Table 3

Deviant Attitudes and Behavior and Cocaine Use

| | Cocaine Use | | | |
| | Men | | Women | |
Attitude or Behavior	Nonuser % (N = 139)	User % (N = 82)	Nonuser % (N = 350)	User % (N = 168)
Very law abidant	30	12***	39	11***
Very liberal	14	30***	13	25***
Very religious	23	19	40	20***
Arrested for drug crime	4	13***	1	5**
Arrested for other crime	8	26***	2	3
Have dealt cocaine	2	23***	0	14***
Drug involved accident	4	5	1	2*
Have used cocaine at work or school	0	26***	0	29***
Good idea to use cocaine	0	20***	1	26***
Trouble with the law	14	35***	3	12***
Trouble with alcohol	6	18***	2	10***
Trouble with drugs	2	17***	2	14***

* $p \leq .05$; ** $p \leq .01$; *** $p \leq .001$.

Table 4

Social Context of Cocaine Use

Context and Variable	----------------Cocaine Use----------------			
	--------Men--------		--------Women-------	
	Nonuser % (N = 139)	User % (N = 82)	Nonuser % (N = 350)	User % (N = 168)
Perceived community approval	7	7	9	15**
Perceived peer approval	6	40***	7	45***
Read drug magazines	4	33***	6	20***
Read drug paraphernalia ads	9	45***	11	24***
Likely to be punished for use	27	18	23	20
Cocaine easy to obtain	59	88***	45	91***

* $p \leq .05$; ** $p \leq .01$; *** $p \leq .001$.

Physical Health

Cocaine users were compared to nonusers in regard to a variety of health status attitudes and behavior. Results of these comparisons are presented in Table 5 separately by sex.

Male cocaine users were more likely to have spent at least one night in the hospital, been seen by a physician for an emergency, felt really sick during the past year, had venereal disease, and less likely to have reported excellent health, compared to male nonusers of cocaine. On the other hand, female cocaine users were more likely to report that their health had deteriorated, had felt really sick in the past year, had venereal disease, and had an abortion, than nonusers of cocaine. These differences indicate that cocaine users reported poorer health statuses than nonusers of cocaine. However, there were no significant differences on eight other health related questions including severe health problems, illness sensitivity, or having been seen by a physician for an illness.

Mental Health

Eight items or scales were used to assess mental health status. Cocaine users were compared to nonusers on each of these variables and the results are presented in Table 6.

Women cocaine users reported ever having a nervous breakdown and psychiatric hospitalization more often than those women who reported no cocaine use. Men did not differ on these two variables.

83

Users were compared to nonusers in regard to four measures of
psychopathology[27] including headache proneness, insomnia, depression, and thought disorder. The upper quartile was used as a dividing
line to define whether these qualities were present, since each was
assessed with multi-item continuous scales. The only significant
difference was that men who used cocaine reported more problems
with insomnia than men who did not use cocaine. The upper quartile
of the magical ideation scale was used to define psychotic proneness.[28] Both men and women cocaine users reported more psychotic
proneness compared to nonusers of cocaine. These results indicate
some small to moderate differences between cocaine users and
nonusers in regard to psychopathology.

Life Satisfaction

Participants were asked to rate their level of happiness or
satisfaction regarding eight different life areas. The percentage of
cocaine users reporting being happy or very happy were compared

Table 5

Physical Health Status and Cocaine Use

Health Status or Event	Men		Women	
	Nonuser % (N = 139)	User % (N = 82)	Nonuser % (N = 350)	User % (N = 168)
Had severe health problems	6	9	9	11
At least one might in hospital	1	5*	9	7
Get sick easy	8	5	16	19
Usually not ill	55	44	44	38
Feel somewhat sick	2	1	7	5
Not as healthy as before	19	28	24	31*
Resistant to illness	82	78	70	69
Health is excellent	87	76*	74	74
Susceptible to illness	11	12	26	26
Seen for emergency	11	22*	18	20
Seen for illness	29	34	46	51
Felt really sick	52	65*	68	76*
Illness sensitive	14	18	30	31
Ever had venereal disease	6	16**	4	10***
You or partner had abortion	4	5	6	10*

* $p \leq .05$; ** $p \leq .01$; *** $p \leq .001$.

Table 6

Mental Health Status of Cocaine Users

| | Cocaine Use | | | |
| | Men | | Women | |
Problem	Nonuser % (N = 139)	User % (N = 82)	Nonuser % (N = 350)	User % (N = 168)
Had nervous breakdown in lifetime	22	22	28	38*
Psychiatric hospitalization	1	1	1	3**
Headache prone	16	15	36	27
Insomnia	18	25*	24	25
Depression	19	21	23	26
Thought disorder	19	17	25	26
Psychotic prone	22	34*	19	33***

* $p \leq .05$; ** $p \leq .01$; *** $p \leq .001$.

with nonusers of each life area. Results of these analyses are presented in Table 7.

Male cocaine users reported less satisfaction with handling emotions, overall health, and accomplishments in life compared to men who did not use cocaine. Women cocaine users reported less satisfaction with intimate relationships and accomplishments in life compared to nonusers of cocaine.

Correlates of Cocaine Use

The foregoing analyses presented important distinctions between those who have and have not used cocaine during the past six months. Another way to examine these effects is to incorporate the intensity or frequency of use. To do this, the quasi-continuous seven-point anchored rating scale for cocaine use has been retained as an indicator of degree of cocaine involvement for the past six months. In the following analyses, this measure was correlated with the variables noted above that were significantly different between users and nonusers. First, simple product-moment correlations are presented, which indicate whether the intensity of use is linearly associated with increases or decreases in the various behaviors or characteristics of the individual. Next, multiple regression analyses are used to select the most important variables that differentiate nonusers and the intensity of use among users, while controlling for common variance among predictor variables. Finally, hierarchical examination of the seven categories of variables are tested for independent prediction of cocaine use and unique impact after controlling for all other variable sets. Whereas in the previous analyses many continuous variables were dichotomized for ease of presentation and interpretation, full scales are used in the following analyses when available.

Bivariate Correlations

Table 8 presents the correlations between level of cocaine use and all variables that were significantly different in the previous analyses. Results are presented separately for men and women.

For the men, all except for seven correlations were significant. Looking at correlations larger than .30, it is apparent that those who were more involved with cocaine also used cigarettes, alcohol, cannabis, hypnotics, stimulants, and psychedelics more frequently, were less law abidant, reported more trouble with the law, had sold more

Table 7

Life Satisfaction and Cocaine Use

	Men		Women	
	Nonuser %	User %	Nonuser %	User %
Life area	(N = 139)	(N = 82)	(N = 350)	(N = 168)
Happy about:				
Handling emotions	84	75*	75	71
Work or school	83	77	74	70
Overall health	91	82*	85	83
Intimate relationship	74	66	71	64*
Enjoyment of life	88	87	86	83
Relationship with family	86	87	81	83
Accomplishments in life	80	67*	72	63*
Sex life	66	69	73	77
Ability to be close	81	78	85	83

* p ≤ .05; ** p ≤ .01; *** p ≤ .001.

Table 8

Bivariate and Multivariate Correlates of Cocaine Use During the
Past Six Months

Predictors	Men Beta[a]	Men r	Women Beta[b]	Women r
High school dropout	.02	.12*	.02	.05
Ever cohabit	.11*	.29***	.00	.27***
Collected unemployment or welfare	.06	.16*	.02	.06
Fired from job	.05	.12*	.01	.14**
Divorced	.01	.06	.03	.10*
Currently cohabiting	.04	.05	.02	.09*
Attending college	-.01	-.18**	.02	-.13**
Have a full-time job	.02	.13*	.02	.15***
Desire a college degree	-.05	-.22***	-.03	-.14**
Nights out with mate/date	.01	.14*	.03	.11*
Frequency of cigarette use	.04	.32***	.07*	.38***
Frequency of alcohol use	.03	.55***	.11***	.48***
Frequency of cannabis use	.34***	.65***	.14***	.55***
Frequency of over-the-counter drug use	.11*	.13*	.00	.22***
Frequency of hypnotic use	.08	.30***	.02	.28***
Frequency of stimulant use	.01	.38***	.13***	.54***
Frequency of psychedelic use	.07	.43***	.02	.38***
Frequency of inhalant use	.00	.09	.06*	.22***
Frequency of narcotic use	.09	.21**	.01	.20***
Frequency of PCP use	.00	.09	.01	.12**
Law abidant	-.03	-.37***	-.02	-.39***
Liberal	.02	.28***	.00	.19***
Religious	.04	-.05	.00	-.21***
Arrested for drug or other crime	.01	.23***	.02	.15***
Trouble with the law	.05	.31***	.00	.21***
Trouble with alcohol or drugs	.06	.29***	.07*	.25***
Drug involved accident	.06	.07	.04	.07*
Amount of cocaine sold	.09	.49***	.09**	.40***
Positive attitude about cocaine use	.34***	.62***	.33***	.71***
Times high on cocaine at work or school	.15**	.52***	.15***	.49***
Perceived community approval for use	.09	.13*	.05	.15***
Perceived peer approval for use	.12*	.56***	.12***	.57***
Times read drug magazine or ads	.08	.40***	.03	.19***
Likelihood of punishment for use	-.07	-.15*	.01	-.16***
Perceived ease of acquisition	.01	.25***	.07**	.41***
Seen doctor for emergency	.06	.15*	.01	.00
Times in hospital	.03	.04	.00	-.03
Have excellent health	-.07	-.19**	.00	-.10*
Ever had veneral disease	.03	.18**	.00	.10*
Self or partner had abortion	.05	.01	.02	.10*
Ever had nervous breakdown	.07	.10	.05	.09*
Ever had psychiatric hospitalization	.07	.03	.04	.09*
Insomnia	.05	.12*	.02	.11*
Psychotic prone	.02	.17**	.03	.17***
Happiness (sum score)	-.03	-.18**	-.01	-.08

[a]$R^2 = .67$, $F = 8.03$***; [b]$R^2 = .70$, $F = 24.86$***
* $p \leq .05$; ** $p \leq .01$; *** $p \leq .001$.

dollars worth of cocaine, had a more positive attitude toward cocaine
use, were high on cocaine more often at work or school, perceived
greater peer approval for use, and had more often read drug magazines and paraphenalia ads. These analyses substantiate those pre-

sented above between users and nonusers and also demonstrate that certain qualities or attitudes become more different with greater cocaine involvement. For the women, all correlations were significant except for five. Those correlations over .30 indicate that greater cocaine involvement was significantly associated with greater use of cigarettes, alcohol, cannabis, stimulants, and psychedelics, less law abidance, having sold more dollars worth of cocaine, a more positive attitude toward cocaine use, having been high on cocaine more times while at work or school, perceived greater peer approval, and found cocaine easier to acquire. Many of these significant correlations are similar to those obtained for the men, and again parallel the user/nonuser differences noted earlier. However, here it can be seen that greater involvement is accompanied by more deviant attitudes and behavior.

Multiple Regression

All variables in Table 8 were simultaneously included as predictors of cocaine involvement in separate equations for men and women. The standardized beta coefficients and their associated significance levels are presented in Table 8.

The equation for the men significantly predicted cocaine involvement and accounted for 67% of the variance in cocaine use. Six predictors made significant and unique contributions to predicting cocaine use. Those who were more involved in cocaine use were more likely to have cohabited, frequently used cannabis and over-the-counter medications, had a very positive attitude toward cocaine use, were often high at work or school on cocaine, and reported greater perceived peer approval for use.

For the women, eleven predictors were significant in the overall equation, which significantly accounted for 70% of the variance in cocaine involvement. Women who used cocaine more frequently were also more likely to have frequently used cigarettes, alcohol, cannabis, stimulants, and inhalants, had more trouble with alcohol or drugs, sold many dollars worth of cocaine, had a very positive attitude toward cocaine use, been frequently high on cocaine at work or school, reported perceived peer approval of use, and found cocaine easy to obtain. Each of these predictors made a significant and unique contribution to understanding the level of cocaine involvement of these women.

Hierarchical Analyses

All variables in Table 8 were grouped into one of seven groups or categories of variables as given in Tables 1 through 7. Each group of variables were used to predict level of cocaine involvement for men and women separately. In addition, the amount of incremental variance for each variable grouping was determined after all other six groups were included. Results of these analyses are summarized in Table 9.

For the men, all variable groupings significantly predicted cocaine use when examined separately. The amount of accountable variance ranged from a low of 5.9% for life satisfaction variables to a high of 52.6% for the deviance variables. However, when the amount of incremental variance was examined, only two groups made a significant contribution over and above the previously included six sets of variables. These variable groupings were other drug use and deviance.

For the women, all variable groupings except life satisfaction significantly predicted frequency of cocaine use when studied separately. The amount of significant accountable variance ranged from a low of 2.2% for the physical health variables to a high of

Table 9

Explained Variance in Young Adult Cocaine Use by
Variable Groups

| Variable Group | Number of Variables | ---------Men--------- | | -------Women-------- | |
		R^2	Incremental[a] R^2	R^2	Incremental R^2
Sociodemographic	11	.173***	.030	.111***	.005
Other drug use	10	.470***	.055***	.543***	.046***
Deviance	12	.526***	.088***	.608***	.094***
Social context	6	.376***	.017	.386***	.015***
Physical health	6	.080**	.010	.022*	.001
Mental health	4	.061**	.008	.029**	.003
Life satisfaction	4	.059**	.003	.008	.002

* $p \leq .05$; ** $p \leq .01$; *** $p \leq .001$.

[a]Additional variance accounted for after entering all other variables.

60.8% for the deviance variables. Three variable groupings made significant increments in accountable variance after controlling for all other variable groups. These variable groups were other drug use, deviance, and social context.

Cocaine Abusers

Although the distinction between use and abuse of psychoactive substances is often difficult to pinpoint, we have decided to consider those who used cocaine one or more times per week during the past six months to be regular users or "abusers." Five percent of the men and 4% of the women in our sample used cocaine this often. Presented in Table 10 is a description of male and female cocaine abusers.

These male cocaine abusers were significantly different from nonusers on 34 variables. Significant differences are indicated in Table 10 and a sample of these differences indicates that male cocaine abusers were more troubled, unhappy, less healthy, heavier users of cigarettes, cannabis, and other substances, more often received public assistance, and were involved in more deviant behavior than nonusers of cocaine. Cocaine abusing women were also quite distinct from women nonusers on 34 variables. A selection of these differences (all of which are given in Table 10) indicate that women cocaine abusers more often had emotional problems, were more frequent users of a variety of substances, had more deviant attitudes, were more involved with deviant behavior, had less job stability, and more likely to be divorced than women who did not use cocaine. Clearly, cocaine abuse has numerous attendant difficulties and problems. These may not all be the result of heavy cocaine use, but are strongly associated with it and the lifestyle of the abuser.

The one unexpected result was that cocaine users and abusers reported both higher income and more frequent work than nonusers. This was particularly evident for women, although there were nonsignificant trends in this direction for men as well. It is possible that those with higher incomes and thus more discretionary income will have greater resources to become involved with cocaine, given the rather costly nature of the drug. And thus, given the opportunity will be more susceptible to cocaine abuse. On the other hand, cocaine abusers were more often on public assistance and had greater trouble keeping a job than nonabusers. These two sets of results seem

Table 10
Description of Cocaine Abusers

Quality or Behavior	-----Cocaine Abuser-----	
	Men %	Women %
Proportion of Sample	5	4
Ever cohabit	70***[a]	55***[a]
Collected unemployment	30**[a]	15
Collected welfare	10***[a]	0
Fired from job	20	35***[a]
Divorced	0	10*[a]
Attending college	10**[b]	20
Have a full-time job	70	80**[a]
Earned more than $15,000	60	45*[a]
Desire a college degree	20***[b]	30**[b]
At least 1 night out/week with mate/date	77*[a]	68*[a]
Use cigarettes	70***[a]	70***[a]
Use alcohol	100	100**[a]
Use cannabis	80***[a]	85***[a]
Use over-the-counter drugs	70	71*[a]
Use hypnotics	30***[a]	33***[a]
Use stimulants	30***[a]	75***[a]
Use psychedelics	50***[a]	30***[a]
Use inhalants	0	15***[a]
Use PCP	0	5*[a]
Very law abidant	10***[b]	9***[b]
Very liberal	50*[a]	50**[a]
Very religious	20	15*[b]
Arrested for drug crime	20*[a]	15***[a]
Arrested for other crime	50***[a]	10***[a]
Trouble with the law	40**[a]	30***[a]
Trouble with alcohol	30**[a]	20***[a]
Trouble with drugs	30**[a]	25***[a]
Have dealt cocaine	60***[a]	40***[a]
Positive attitude about cocaine use	20**[a]	40***[a]
Have used cocaine at work or school	60***[a]	60***[a]
Perceived community approval	20*[a]	20*[a]
Perceived peer approval	70***[a]	60***[a]
Read drug magazines	30***[a]	35***[a]
Read drug paraphenalia ads	50***[a]	30**[a]
Cocaine easy to obtain	100***[a]	100***[a]
Seen for emergency	30*[a]	25
At least one night in hospital	20***[a]	0
Health is excellent	60**[b]	80
Resistant to illness	60*[b]	70
Had nervous breakdown in lifetime	0	50**[a]
Headache prone	0*[b]	50
Psychotic prone	20	45***[a]
Happy about health	70**[b]	90
Happy about enjoyment of life	71*[b]	84
Happy about accomplishments in life	40**[b]	70

*p ≤ .05; ** p ≤ .01; *** p ≤ .001.
[a] Significantly higher percentage than nonusers.
[b] Significantly lower percentage than nonusers.

contradictory, unless dealing cocaine or other drugs provided a comfortable income for the cocaine users. This is supported by the fact that large percentages of cocaine users and abusers have also sold cocaine.

Longitudinal Prediction of Changes in Cocaine Use

Fifteen personality measures,[25] eight health and psychological functioning scales,[27] and four social support variables assessed in 1980 were used to predict changes in cocaine use from 1980 to 1984. Separate analyses were run for men and women. Multiple regression analyses were used with young adult cocaine use as the dependent variable. Adolescent (1980) use of cocaine was entered as the first predictor variable, and the other 27 predictors were entered in a stepwise manner based on their amount of independent contribution to predicting young adult cocaine use. For the men, four variables, in addition to adolescent cocaine use, predicted young adult cocaine use (Multiple $R = .60$, $R^2 = .36$, $F = 20.83$, $p \leq .001$). These variables indicated that increased cocaine use for that four-year period was predicted from adolescent lack of law abidance, lack of diligence, more generosity, and lack of headache proneness. Two variables were selected, in addition to adolescent cocaine use, in order to predict significantly young adult cocaine use for the women (Multiple $R = .56$, $R^2 = .31$, $F = 68.27$, $p \leq .001$). Substantively, these variables indicated that a lack of law abidance and more attractiveness were predictive of increased cocaine use for women over this four year period.

DISCUSSION

From all accounts, cocaine use has become relatively widespread among all segments of society.[2-4,29] In this current sample, 37% of the men and 32% of the women have used cocaine at least once during the past six months. If this sample can be generalized to other young adults, then one in every three individuals in their early twenties has tried cocaine. Along with cannabis and stimulants, cocaine has become the most frequently used illicit drug among the young.[4] Data from the most recent 1982 national household survey indicated that 28% of 18 to 25 year olds had tried cocaine sometime in their life, and 18% had tried it during the past year.[29] Although the household survey results indicated lower prevalence rates than those reported in the current sample, it must be remembered that their sample included younger participants and data were obtained two years earlier than those reported here.

Given the prevalence of cocaine use, it is surprising that so few studies have examined the psychosocial context of its use and the type(s) of persons who become involved with or even try it. An exception to this paucity is an in-depth analysis of nine cocaine users.[30] These cocaine users all utilized the drug as a means of escape from some uncomfortable life condition. For these subjects, cocaine "provides a ticket to another reality, where life is pleasant and troubles are few." To the question of why cocaine and not any other type of drug, the researchers suggest that "cocaine may well provide . . . the ecstasy that is missing in modern life that so many people genuinely seem to need." The nine participants had serious relationship problems with their fathers and other intimate contacts with the opposite sex. Many had trouble dealing with responsibilities of ordinary life and the heavy users felt that cocaine "can make you crazy and paranoid as hell." Other chronic effects of cocaine use have been noted and include insomnia, irritability, anxiety, rhinitis, other nasal problems, weight loss, attentional or perceptual disturbances, and lassitude.[19,21,31]

Results from this current study of many young adults contribute substantial data to understanding the type of person who is involved with cocaine. Clear distinctions emerged between users and nonusers, wtih differences becoming more apparent with greater involvement. For men, the biggest differences were on deviant behaviors and use of other drug substances. Those men who used cocaine were significantly more likely to use all types of licit and illicit drugs than nonusers of cocaine. Similar results were apparent for women cocaine users. Both men and women cocaine users were also significantly more likely to hold deviant or nontraditional attitudes and to have been involved in deviant or problem behavior, than those who have not used cocaine. Another powerful influence, most notable among the women, was the immersion in a social context conducive to cocaine use. For instance, perceived peer and community approval, ease of acquisition, and exposure to drug oriented media were strongly associated with greater cocaine involvement.

In general, those who were involved with cocaine were less successful at traditional adult roles and participated more in nonconforming behaviors. For instance, cocaine users were more likely to be divorced, have dropped out of high school, be less interested and involved with college pursuits, have cohabited without marriage, and been fired from a job. It is unclear whether these differences preceded, were a consequence of, or simply were associated with cocaine use. However, cocaine users have created lifestyles that are nontraditional, deviant, and often at odds with society. They are more likely to be involved with both licit and illicit drugs, perceive themselves as more liberal and less law abidant, to be more involved in criminal activity and have greater trouble with the law, and to live in a social context that is conducive to use of illegal substances.

Whether as an antecedent, consequence, or simply concomitant of cocaine use, users reported more physical and mental health problems than nonusers. In regard to emotional difficulties, male cocaine users reported more insomnia and psychotic proneness (as measured by amount of magic ideation) than nonusers, whereas female cocaine users were more likely to report nervous breakdowns, psychiatric hospitalizations, and psychotic proneness than nonusers. Drug abusers' greater psychotic proneness or tendencies have been noted in other research,[32] as well as their greater utilization of psychiatric services.[2] Although not significant in the current findings, previous research has noted that depression significantly increased cocaine use among adolescents over a one-year period,[5] a finding that is consistent with cocaine treatment research which has found that abstinence from cocaine is more likely when the patient was treated with tricyclic antidepressants.[33] Apparently a certain group of cocaine users may be medicating true psychiatric symptomatology and not just simply be involved in deviant or noncomformist behavior. Our finding that women cocaine users have had more hospitalizations and nervous breakdowns than nonusers supports this hypothesis.

In regard to physical illness, cocaine users reported slightly poorer health status, less health satisfaction, and greater utilization of treatment resources than nonusers. It is impossible to determine precisely whether this association is a direct result of cocaine use. However, other research has indicated that there may be health compromising consequences to cocaine abuse.[19,21]

Finally, the quality of life or life satisfaction seems less for cocaine users compared to nonusers. This is more apparent for men than women. Male cocaine users reported less happiness with handling their feelings (emotional difficulties), their overall health, and what they were accomplishing in life, than nonusers. Women cocaine users reported less satisfaction with their intimate relationships and their accomplishments in life than nonusers. Although significant, these differences were relatively small, but may indicate that cocaine users have greater general psychological distress compared to nonusers.[34]

Finally, several personality, but not health and psychological functioning nor social support, variables predicted significant increases of cocaine use from adolescence to young adulthood. A lack of law abidance or social conformity was the strongest predictor for men and women. Other important variables for the men included a lack of diligence, more generosity, and a lack of headache susceptibility. For the women, the only other variable, besides a lack of law abidance, to lead to increased cocaine use was more perceived attractiveness. Interestingly, none of the social support or health and psychological functioning variables (i.e., depression, thought disorder, insomnia) predicted changes in cocaine use as would be expected from previous research.[5,35]

Overall, some clear and distinct differences were found between cocaine users and nonusers in this sample of young adults. Many differences increased with greater involvement with the drug, to the point where cocaine abusers were quite dissimilar to nonusers. The hazards and severe psychological dependencies associated with cocaine are increasingly apparent and it is becoming imperative to have a clear and concise understanding of the type of individual who is involved with its use. Towards this goal this study has been directed.

REFERENCES

1. Adams EH, Durell J: Cocaine: A growing public health problem, in Grabowski J (ed.): *Cocaine: Pharmacology, effects, and treatment of abuse.* Rockville, MD, National Institute on Drug Abuse, 1984, pp. 9–14.

2. Pope HG, Ionescu-Pioggia M, Cole JO: Drug use and life style among college undergraduates: Nine years later. *Arch Gen Psychiatry* 1981;38:588–591.

3. Johnston LD, O'Malley PM, Bachman JG: *Drugs and American high school students: 1975–1983.* Rockville, MD, National Institute on Drug Abuse, 1981.

4. Johnston LD, O'Malley PM, Bachman JG: *Use of licit and illicit drugs by American high school students: 1975–1983.* Rockville, MD, National Institute on Drug Abuse, 1985.

5. Newcomb MD, Bentler PM: Cocaine use among adolescents: Longitudinal associations with social context, psychopathology, and use of other substances. *Addict Behav,* 1986;11:263–273.

6. Kandel DB, Logan JA: Periods of risk for initiation, stabilization, and decline in drug use from adolescence to early adulthood. *Am J Public Health* 1984;74:660–666.

7. Newcomb MD, Bentler PM: Substance use from adolescence to young adulthood: Stability and change. Paper presented at the American Psychological Association, Los Angeles, California, (1985, August).

8. Adams EH: Abuse/availability trends of cocaine in the United States. *Drug Surveillance Reports*, Vol. 1, Rockville, MD, National Institute on Drug Abuse, 1982.

9. Blanken AJ, Adams EH, Durell J: Drug Abuse: Implications and current trends. *Psychiatric Medicine*, in press.

10. Kozel NJ, Crider RA, Adams EH: National surveillance of cocaine use and related health consequences. *Morbidity and Mortality Weekly Report 31* 1982;20:265–273. (Center for Disease Control, Atlanta, GA)

11. Jones RT: Cocaine and stimulants. In *Drug abuse and drug abuse research*. Rockville, MD, National Institute on Drug Abuse, 1984a.

12. Glatt MM: *A guide to addiction and its treatment*. New York, Wiley and Sons Inc., 1973.

13. Fischman MW, Schuster CR: Acute tolerance to cocaine in humans, in Harris LS (ed.): *Problems of drug dependence, 1980*. Rockville, MD, National Institute on Drug Abuse, 1981.

14. Siegel RK: Cocaine smoking. *J Psychoactive Drugs* 1982;14:271–359.

15. Hunt DE, Strug DL, Goldsmith DS, Lipton DS, Spunt B, Truitt L, Robertson KA: An instant shot of "Aah": Cocaine use among methadone clients. *J Psychoactive Drugs* 1984;16:217–227.

16. Post RM, Kopanda RT, Black KE: Progressive effects of cocaine on behavior and central amine metabolism in rhesus monkeys: Relationship to kindling and psychoses. *Biological Psychiatry* 1976;11:403–419.

17. Jones RT: The pharmacology of cocaine, in Grabowski J (ed.): *Cocaine: Pharmacology, effects, and treatment of abuse*. Rockville, MD, National Institute on Drug Abuse, 1984b, pp. 34–53.

18. Mills CJ, Noyes HL: Patterns and correlates of initial and subsequent drug use among adolescents. *J Consult Clin Psychol* 1984;52:231–243.

19. Siegel RK: Changing patterns of cocaine use: Longitudinal observations, consequences, and treatment, in Grabowski J (ed.): *Cocaine: Pharmacology, effects, and treatment of abuse*. Rockville, MD, National Institute on Drug Abuse, 1984.

20. Musto DF: A study in cocaine: Sherlock Holmes and Sigmund Freud. *JAMA* 1968;204:27–32.

21. Grinspoon L, Bakalar JB: *Cocaine: A drug and its social evolution*. New York, Basic Books, 1976.

22. Egan DJ, Robinson DO: Cocaine: Magical drug or menace? *Int J Addict* 1979; 14:231–241.

23. Fischman MW: The behavioral pharmacology of cocaine in humans, in Grabowski J (ed.): *Cocaine: Pharmacology, effects, and treatment of abuse*. Rockville, MD, National Institute on Drug Abuse, 1984, pp. 72–91.

24. Kandel DB: Marijuana users in young adulthood. *Arch Gen Psychiatry* 1984;41:200–209.

25. Huba GJ, Bentler PM: A developmental theory of drug use: Derivation and assessment of a causal modeling approach, in Baltes BP, Brim OG Jr. (eds.): *Life-span development and behavior, volume 4*. New York, Academic Press, 1982.

26. Newcomb, MD: Nuclear attitudes and reactions: Associations with depression, drug use, and quality of life. *J Personal Soc Psychol*, 1986;50:906–920.

27. Newcomb MD, Huba GJ, Bentler PM: A multidimensional assessment of stressful events among adolescents: Derivation and correlates. *J Heal Soc Behav* 1981;22:400–415.

28. Eckblad M, Chapman LJ: Magical ideation as an indicator of schizotypy. *J Consult Clin Psycho* 1983;51:215–225.

29. Cisin I, Miller J. Abelson H: *The national household survey on drug abuse 1982*. Rockville, MD, National Institute on Drug Abuse, 1983.

30. Spotts JV, Shontz FC: *The lifestyles of nine American cocaine users: Trips to the land of cockaigne*. Rockville, MD, National Institute on Drug Abuse, 1976.

31. Siegel RK: Long-term effects of recreational cocaine use: A four year study, in Jeri FR (ed.): *Cocaine 1980*. Lima, Pacific Press, 1980, pp. 11-16.

32. Tsuang MT, Simpson JC, Kronfol Z: Subtypes of drug abuse with psychosis. *Arch Gen Psychiatry* 1982;39:141-147.

33. Gawin FH, Kleber HD: Cocaine abuse treatment: Open pilot trial with desipramine and lithium carbonate, *Arch Gen Psychiatry* 1984;41:903-909.

34. Tanaka JS, Huba GJ: Confirmatory hierarchical factor analyses of psychological distress measures. *J Personal Soc Psychol* 1984;46:621-635.

35. Khantzian EJ, Khantzian NJ: Cocaine addiction: Is there a psychological predisposition? *Psychiatr Annals* 1984;14:753-759.

Cocaine Use in Persons on Methadone Maintenance

R. Hanbury, PhD
V. Sturiano, PhD
M. Cohen, MD
B. Stimmel, MD
C. Aguillaume, MD

ABSTRACT. Although cocaine use had increased dramatically among all levels of society over the past several years, its use by heroin addicts has existed for decades. To determine whether the prevalence or the pattern of cocaine use changes once an addict enrolls in methadone maintenance, a survey of cocaine use among persons in methadone maintenance therapy was conducted.

Of the 613 persons surveyed, 229 (37%) chose to participate, with 33 (14%) considered invalid because of incomplete responses. Of the remaining 196 (86% of the participants), 64 (33%) indicated no cocaine use prior to methadone maintenance, and 132 (67%) reported some prior use. Once treatment had begun, 9 (14%) with no history of prior use admitted to at least one event within the last 6 months, and 55 (86%) reported no use. Of those reporting use prior to methadone maintenance, 41 (31%) stopped usage and 91 (69%) continued. Of the total participants, approximately half used cocaine at least once during methadone maintenance. Among those who used cocaine before and during methadone maintenance, the predominant route of administration was parenteral, 72 (54%) and 46 (51%) participants, respectively. It should be noted that there was a net gain of 17% of patients who stopped using cocaine as a result of entering methadone maintenance. Indices of cocaine use by random urinalysis over the preceding 6 months, for the entire clinic population, revealed only 86 (14%) to 110 (18%) patients to have urine samples positive for cocaine.

Although cocaine use decreased on methadone maintenance, its use is still considerable, with the pattern of use differing from the recreational cocaine use in a non-narcotic-dependent population.

R. Hanbury, V. Sturiano, M. Cohen, B. Stimmel, and C. Aguillaume are affiliated with the Department of Medicine and Psychiatry, Mount Sinai School of Medicine and Psychiatry, of New York, NY.

Random urinalysis for cocaine appears to be an insensitive indicator of prevalence of use.

Attitudes toward cocaine use have changed considerably since the drug was first introduced in the United States in the late 19th Century. Initially, cocaine was a status symbol and its use was glamorized by jetsetters, celebrities, sports and entertainment figures.[1] Over the past several years, however, the use of this drug among the general population, has profoundly increased. A 1982 National Institute of Drug Abuse survey of American households found that 21.6 million Americans, some one in ten of the total population, had tried cocaine, with almost 12 million using it in the year preceding the survey. There were approximately 4.2 million people consuming the drug at least once a month.[2]

Cocaine use by heroin addicts, however, is far from a new phenomenon. Although frequently used independently of heroin, often small amounts of cocaine are mixed with the heroin and then injected. This combination, termed a "speedball," is felt to decrease the time that an addict would be "on the nod," thereby making him less susceptible to arrest, as well as providing a pleasurable rush immediately after injection. Parenteral use of cocaine has thus become part of the lifestyle of the heroin addict and, with some individuals, especially those with a tolerance to the euphoric effects of heroin, may be the primary reason for continuing injection. Once enrolled on methadone maintenance (MM), whether an individual's consumption of cocaine will continue, will decrease or become more similar to cocaine use in the general population remains unclear. Although cocaine and its metabolites can be detected in the urine, the ability of urinalysis to regularly detect cocaine use remains unclear.

To determine the change in prevalence and pattern of cocaine use in heroin addicts, subsequent to enrolling in MM, a survey of cocaine use among persons enrolled in MM was undertaken. The initial hypotheses of this survey were:

1. the amount of cocaine used by patients in MM would be less than that used while dependent on heroin. This hypothesis is based on the assumption that counseling and support services would address all patterns of chemical dependency.
2. the pattern of use would be recreational rather than parenteral, thereby similar to the non-heroin dependent population; and
3. urinalysis would be an insensitive indicator of cocaine use.

This statement is based upon the findings of representative research which indicates that urine and plasma levels can be detected up to eight hours for cocaine and twenty-four hours for the metabolite, benzoylecgonine.[3] Clearly, the probability of detecting a rapidly metabolized substance with a short biologic half-life is lessened when random selection procedures are used for urine sampling. In order to detect the presence of this substance, it would be necessary to submit frequent urine specimens for toxicology screenings. If by clinical observation patients were suspected of abusing this substance, or other drug(s), they would be required to submit a urine specimen at that time. Such specimens were in addition to the randomized submissions.

METHODS

An anonymous questionnaire, addressing patterns of cocaine use before and during MM, was distributed to 613 persons enrolled in a MM treatment program. The clinic is a large hospital based methadone maintenance program and is strictly voluntary. It is a state funded program where approximately 56% of the clinic population are on medicaid and the remaining patients are fee paying members. The specific parameters reviewed in the questionnaire were:

1. the presence or absence of cocaine use during periods of heroin addiction, prior to MM; and
2. the presence or absence of cocaine use within 180 days from the time of the survey or while in MM.

Positive responses were categorized by use of cocaine alone or in combination with heroin and by the route of administration. Objective evidence of cocaine use by analysis of random urine specimens during the six-month period was also determined.

RESULTS

Of the 613 persons receiving the questionnaire, 229 (37%) responded. Of these responses, 33 (14%) were incomplete andconsidered invalid. The remaining 196 (86%) responses were used for final analyses. Participation was completely voluntary. The only positive reinforcement was encouragement by staff to assist in the collection of information which might be helpful in the development of strategies to deal with the cocaine problem, e.g., specialized group intervention. Despite reassurances of anonymity, a common attitude appeared to be that self-disclosure would compromise "take-out" privileges or methadone dosage. The lack of immediate, tangible reinforcement and defensiveness about voluntarily revealing patterns of drug use might be factors contributing to the low response rate.

Of these 196 responders, 64 (33%) indicated that they had not used cocaine while dependent on heroin. Of this group, 55 (86%) continued to refrain from cocaine use during enrollment in MM. Nine (14%) of these individuals did, however, initiate cocaine use at least once during this period (Table I).

Cocaine use, while on heroin, was reported in 132 (67%) cases, with 91 (69%) continuing cocaine use subsequent to initiating MM. Of the 100 patients (51%) using cocaine at least once while on MM, only 9 (14%) used this drug for the first time after enrolling in treatment. A significant difference existed between cocaine use prior to being in treatment and use once treatment had been initiated (p < .001).

Patterns of cocaine use, however, were only slightly affected by enrollment in MM, with free-basing becoming more prominent but not statistically significant. Of the 132 persons using cocaine prior to treatment, 72 (55%) mainlined cocaine, 15 (11%) sniffed and one (0.08%) free-based, with 44 (33%) using multiple routes. Subsequent to the initiation of MM, only 46 (51%) mainlined, 26 (29%) sniffed, 5 (6%) free-based and 14 (15%) used multiple routes (Table II).

Indices of cocaine use by random urinalyses for 613 persons enrolled in MM revealed only 86 (14%) to 110 (18%) to have had positive findings. The randomization system is based on two components; namely, patients who were consistently negative in their toxicology screenings for six months were randomly selected on a monthly basis; patients who abused a substance, whether objectively reported or clinically observed, were randomly selected on a weekly basis.

Of the 196 patients agreeing to participate in the study, 66 (34%) had urines positive for cocaine, with cocaine as the sole drug in 14 (7%) and in combination with heroin in 52 (27%) (Table III).

TABLE I. Cocaine Abuse: Pre- and During MM Treatment

	COCAINE USE PRIOR MM		NO COCAINE USE PRIOR MM		TOTAL	
	NO. PTS.	%	NO. PTS.	%	NO. PTS.	%
COCAINE USE IN 6 MONTHS MM PERIOD	91	(69)	9	(14)	100	(51)
NO COCAINE USE IN 6 MONTHS MM PERIOD	41	(31)	55	(86)	96	(49)
TOTAL	132	(100)	64	(100)	196	(100)

TABLE II. Routes of Administration: Pre- and During MM Treatment

ROUTES OF ADMINISTRATION	COCAINE USE PRIOR MM		COCAINE USE DURING MM	
	NO. PTS	%	NO. PTS.	%
MAINLINED	72	(55)	46	(51)
SNIFFED	15	(11)	26	(29)
FREEBASED	1	(0.8)	5	(6)
SKIN-POPPED	0	(--)	0	(--)
MULTIPLE ROUTES	44	(33)	14	(15)
TOTAL	132	(100)	91	(100)

TABLE III. Pattern of Use During Treatment

DRUGS	TOXICOLOGY REPORTS #	TOXICOLOGY REPORTS %	SELF-REPORT #	SELF-REPORT %
COCAINE	14	(7)	64	(33)
SPEEDBALL (COCAINE & HEROIN)	52	(27)	37	(19)
HEROIN ONLY	27	(14)	--*	--*
NEGATIVE	103	(53)	95	(49)
TOTAL	196	(100)	196	(100)

* NOT ASKED IN SURVEY

DISCUSSION

Although cocaine may be taken in a variety of ways among recreational users, the common mode is snorting, or, for the real aficionados, free-basing. Intravenous injection is quite rare.[4] The results of this survey indicate that the use of cocaine by persons in MM differs from general recreational patterns and is considerable, with up to 50% continuing to inject this drug. The incidence of cocaine use in MM is somewhat more than that reported by Hunt et al., who found 36% of methadone patients to have used cocaine at least once in the week prior to the survey, with usage varying between cohorts in treatment from a low of 19% in those patients whose urines were negative for other drugs to a high of 82% in those also using heroin.[5] In our study, the use of cocaine with heroin is quite prevalent, being noted in 79% of all urines positive for cocaine. Although cocaine use significantly decreased while on MM, it still is of considerable prevalence and, not surprisingly, is related to heroin use.

Although the desire to use heroin is significantly reduced with MM, the cross-tolerance induced by methadone is effective only with other narcotics. Since anxiety is frequently a contributing factor toward initiation of heroin dependence, institution of methadone maintenance may cause the anxiety of heroin dependence to resurface, resulting in the use of other mood-altering drugs. Although alcohol is probably among the least expensive agents, its prevalence among patients in MM is less than that seen for cocaine use.[6] This may be related to a number of factors, including the association of cocaine with a specific status, the conditioning effects that prior use of cocaine has on reinforcing subsequent use in order to relieve anxiety and its ready availability in every neighborhood at what has now become relatively low cost.

Detection of cocaine use is often not easy. Frequently, with regular heavy use, a recognizable clinical syndrome, consisting of weight loss and fatigue, will appear. Less frequent use will only be detected through self-admission or urinalysis. The most common method of urinalysis performed in methadone programs, thin-layer chromatography, is sensitive to the presence of cocaine and its metabolites. It's utility, however, is effected by factors such as the short half-life of cocaine in the human body and, in the case of this study, randomly obtained urine samples.

Although cocaine had previously been considered a rather benign recreational drug, in fact, its continued use at high doses is associated with both adverse psychological and medical effects.[3,5,7] The risks of cocaine use among persons in MM are of particular concern. Since the pattern of use for the most part resembles that most often seen in heroin dependency, the conditioning effects experienced through recurrent injections of cocaine may keep alive the need for injection and the desire to inject heroin. This is probably responsible for continuing heroin injection despite being on a methadone dose sufficient to prevent narcotic-induced euphoria. Parenteral injection of cocaine carries with it the risks associated with heroin injection. The hypermetabolic state associated with cocaine use may also interfere with the metabolism of methadone, as well as promote the use of antidepressant drugs and tranquilizers in an attempt to come down off a high or to maintain a relative equilibrium.[5] As documented by Hunt et al., cocaine use is also associated with considerable alcohol and heroin use. Finally, although the cost of cocaine has decreased somewhat due to its ready availability, nonetheless, for individuals on marginal incomes, this expense becomes critical. As a result, there may be a marked decrease in lifestyle, as well as an urge to engage in criminal activity in order to support one's habit.

It should be noted that although prevalence of cocaine use in this study was considerable, the study design may not allow for a definitive statement to be made concerning such use. Even though participation was voluntary, self-reporting raises questions of reliability. In addition, the variable of time in treatment was not controlled which, in turn, may provide a somewhat inflated estimate of cocaine use once in MM.

In summary, cocaine use among persons in MM, although significantly decreased from that seen during a period of active heroin addiction, is nonetheless considerable and often associated with continued use of heroin, thereby exposing the user to all of the medical complications that had been associated with prior heroin use. It is a problem which appears to be increasing and must be addressed in order to provide the most optimal rehabilitation for the former heroin use.

REFERENCES

1. Cohen, S. "Recent developments in the abuse of cocaine". Bulletin on Narcotics. 1984, XXXVI(2):1–14
2. Gold, M. S. *800-Cocaine*, New York: Bantam Books, 1984.
3. Mule, S.J. The Pharmacodynamics of cocaine abuse. Psychiatric Annals. 1984; 14(10): 724–727.

4. Winick, C. The sociology of cocaine. In: *Proceedings of Symposium of Cocaine.* New York: New York State Division of Substance Abuse Services, 1983.

5. Hunt D., Strug, D., Goldsmith, D., Lipton, D., Spunt, B., Truitt, L. and Robertson, K. An instant shot of "Aah": cocaine use among methadone clients. Journal of Psychoactive Drugs. 1984; 16(3): 217–227.

6. Carroll, J., Malloy, T. and Kendrich, R. Alcohol abuse by drug dependent persons: A literature review. American Journal of Drug and Alcohol Abuse Services. 1977; 4(8): 293–315.

7. Morningstar, P. Cocaine user subculture. In: *Proceedings of Symposium on Cocaine.* New York: New York State Division of Substance Abuse Services, 1983.

The Costly Bonus:
Cocaine Related Crime
Among Methadone Treatment Clients

Dana Hunt
Barry Spunt
Douglas Lipton
Douglas Goldsmith
David Strug

ABSTRACT. This paper examines the relationship between the use of cocaine and criminal activity among 368 current methadone maintenance clients and 142 narcotics users not in treatment. Findings include an increase of cocaine use among methadone clients in the last ten years and the indication that cocaine plays an increasingly important role in the criminal activity of both methadone clients and users not in treatment. We find a direct relationship between escalating use of cocaine and increasing involvement in crime. The relationship is related to properties of the drug itself, its costs and the lifestyle associated with cocaine use.

INTRODUCTION

While the relationship between narcotics use and crime has been exhaustively examined, research on cocaine use has focused primarily on its psychological, historical and physiological effects[1-5] and only recently on its relationship to crime. This may be due in part to an image of cocaine as "the rich man's drug",[1] whose users are wealthy enough to support their use without resorting to crime. The only historical exception was the period earlier in this century

This research was supported by a grant from the National Institute on Drug Abuse (1 H81 DA 02300-01) to Narcotics and Drug Research, Inc., New York and the Division of Substance Abuse Services, New York State. Opinions expressed in this paper do not necessarily reflect policy of the NIDA or the Division of Substance Abuse Services. This paper was originally presented at the Annual Meeting of the American Society of Criminology, November, 1983, Denver, CO.

when cocaine was associated with minority groups who were portrayed as physically powerful and prone to violence while under the influence of cocaine, a "devil drug".[6-8]

In the 1970s, cocaine became increasingly popular among all classes in society, eroding its traditional boundaries of a small number of upper income users and the narcotic addict population.[4,9-11] A 1981 survey of New York State households reports cocaine as the third most commonly used drug (after marijuana and stimulants), indicating a three-fold increase in use since a similar statewide survey in 1976.[12] The increased use spans all income categories. Three percent of those earning less than $15,000 and 6% of those earning less than $25,000 reported the use of cocaine in the previous month. Few of these users can simply be characterized as narcotics addicts; in fact, 10% used no other drugs besides cocaine and 35% used only cocaine and marijuana.

There are also increasing reports linking cocaine use to criminal activity.[11,13] In a survey of 500 cocaine users, the majority of whom were working professionals, Gold[11] finds that 25% of his sample resorted to theft from work to gain money for the drug. Morningstar[14] reports that crime is the best predictor of level of use, and 26% of high level users in her sample reported that they had stolen something from family or friends to obtain money for cocaine; 52% of these high level users were also regularly involved in trafficking cocaine. Criminal activity among users is related to both the cost of cocaine and its unique physiological action. A gram of cocaine can cost from $75-120 with users reporting an almost unlimited ceiling of use.[8] Since its effects are short-lived and the depression which follows heavy use encourages continued use, enormous quantities of the drug can be consumed in a "run" or extended period of use.[15,16]

This paper examines the relationship between cocaine use and criminal activity in a group of methadone maintenance clients, persons whose average income level makes the additional expense of cocaine use an almost immediate financial problem. This group is not typical of the cocaine user naive to either drugs or criminal activity. Thirty-three percent of this sample report that they had at one time used cocaine heavily and the majority have had some experience with the criminal justice system.[17] They are a fascinating group, however, for these very reasons. First, many are financially comparable to middle to lower income cocaine users whose use may come to exceed their ability to afford it. Secondly, they, unlike most other middle to lower income users, are persons with developed illegal skills. These skills, developed during or concurrent with heroin addiction, may be drawn upon more easily and surface more readily than the illegal resources available to persons naive to crime. Consequently, a relationship between extensive use of cocaine and criminal activity may be more quickly apparent in the more experienced treatment population than in other users.

METHODS

These data are derived from the Tri-State Ethnographic Project (TRISEP) interview and ethnographic materials. Data collection was carried out over an eighteen month period (1981–1982) at four research sites in three states. The four sites, methadone maintenance treatment programs, were selected in cooperation with the Single State Agencies of each state on the basis of matching demographic characteristics of clients, the presence of common clinic problems (such as diversion, polydrug use and alcohol use of clients) and for their willingness to participate in the research.

Current methadone clients at each site were trained as field-work guides for the researchers to the client and narcotics users not in treatment communities. These seven workers were persons with extensive and recent experiences with heroin addiction and were able to move freely in both the client and addict world. They were trained in observation and interview techniques and conducted the initial life history interview with all respondents. They also made taped weekly observation reports from field journals and notes carried during their week of interviewing and observation.

Subjects

The sample consists of 510 subjects, 368 who are currently in methadone treatment and 142 who are not currently in treatment but who are active users of heroin and cocaine.[A] Forty-four percent of the methadone client sample were randomly selected from the four clinic rolls for the interviews. The other 56% were clients who came forward offering to be interviewed. Some of the non-random clients were persons the researchers actively sought, such as clients just entering treatment, clients undergoing detoxification or pregnant clients. The randomly generated and the self-selected groups were analyzed for comparability and found not to differ significantly on a number of demographic and behavioral variables and are combined in this analysis.

The sample of persons not in treatment was obtained through the efforts of the client fieldworkers. Each fieldworker was instructed to seek acquaintances who were still using heroin, persons in the clinic area buying methadone and persons in the drug dealing and drug using areas of each city. This sample is a purposive sample; it is comparable to those reported by other researchers of addiction in terms of drug activity and background characteristics of respondents, but inferences cannot be generalized to the addict population as a whole. They are examined only briefly in this paper for comparative purposes.

All respondents were voluntary and were paid for interview time. All were protected by the use of code names and numbers, and no information about them was shared with clinic staff, other clients or any local agencies. Table 1 provides a summary of the characteristics of subjects.

Data Collection

This analysis is based on extensive interviewing conducted in the areas of the four methadone maintenance programs studied. Two structured interviews, totaling approximately two hours duration, were conducted in the treatment facility in a private room provided or outside of the clinic in a car, a diner or on a nearby park bench. Both clients and addicts not in treatment often preferred to be interviewed outside of the clinic proper to insure confidentiality. The interviews covered a wide range of topics: criminal activity, treatment history, drug history, employment history, attitudes toward treatment, family background, current living arrangement, drug and alcohol use.

The data also include many hours of taped observation and field reports from each area. Researchers and fieldworkers spent many hours ''hanging out'' in the clinic areas talking to clients and staff. Their interviews, conversations and field notes were taped and transcribed for analysis.

TABLE 1: Characteristics of In treatment and Not In Treatment subjects

	N=368 In Treatment	N=142 Not In Treatment
Race		
White	50% (182)	40% (57)
Black	37% (137)	53% (75)
Hispanic	13% (46)	6% (8)
Other	1% (3)	1% (2)
Sex		
Male	64% (235)	70% (99)
Female	35% (133)	30% (43)
Age		
Under 20	* (1)	4% (5)
21-30 yrs.	56% (205)	68% (96)
31-40 yrs.	37% (136)	24% (34)
40 yrs. or older	7% (25)	5% (7)
Education		
Less than 6 yrs.	1% (4)	1% (1)
7-9 yrs.	16% (58)	35% (50)
10-12 yrs.	64% (237)	57% (81)
More than 12 yrs.	19% (69)	7% (10)
Employment		
Employed	31% (115)	35% (49)
Unemployed	69% (253)	65% (93)

*Less than 1%

Definition of Variables

The report of individual crimes were used separately to determine the frequency of commission of particular types of crime and combined to determine the overall amount of criminal activity. The variable, *property crime*, consists of the sum of the frequencies of committing any of the following non-drug dealing, acquisitive crimes in the two week period prior to the interview: burglary, robbery, shoplifting (own use and for resale), dealing stolen merchandise, prostitution, forgery, con games, dealing in stolen merchandise and some participation in illegal business such as numbers running. The variable, *drug dealing crime*, is a similar summation of the frequency of dealing any of the following drugs in the prior two week period: heroin, methadone, other opiate, cocaine, marijuana, barbiturates, amphetamines, tranquilizers and sedatives or any other drug such as PCP. In addition, drug dealing includes steering or touting drugs for either money or drugs. Steering involves directing or taking a buyer to a seller for a money or drug cut of the sale. Touting involves a type of advertising or hawking a particular dealer's products in exchange for either money or drugs.

Drug use is defined as the self report of the frequency of the use of any of nine categories of drugs in the week prior to the interview. As with the self report of criminal activity, we had to rely to the respondents honesty with some assistance from the knowledge of the fieldworkers and observations. Urinalysis data are available on the sample of the methadone clients.[B] However, these data do not provide daily or current drug use information needed.

There are several limitations to these data. First, the problems associated with self report data are not resolved by this research design. However, the use of indigenous fieldworkers combined with extensive field observation aid in the validation of reported data. For example, an individual who reports no criminal activity in the week prior to the interview, but is daily selling drugs in the clinic area can be prompted for a more accurate answer or eliminated as an unreliable source. Secondly, because the four programs were not randomly selected, the sample of methadone clients, while representative of respective clinics, may not necessarily be representative of methadone clients in general.

RESULTS

Cocaine's increased popularity in the general population is reflected in its increased use among methadone clients. TRISEP data indicate that cocaine is a drug of high status among methadone clients, even those who may use no other drugs. Like users in the general population, methadone clients who use cocaine often view it as a drug whose use indicates upward mobility, a drug which makes the user feel "all dressed up." Cocaine is available to this population in units costing $5 and $10, making it more affordable than popular media accounts of cocaine use lead one to expect. The client using cocaine once or twice a week is not a "high roller" buying $100 grams of cocaine, but is rather purchasing "nickel" ($5) or "dime" ($10) bags, often for injection as well as insufflation.

Increase of Cocaine Use

Cocaine use among methadone clients is significantly more common than reported in similar treatment populations studied in the early 1970s. Taylor et al.,[18] found that 19% of their methadone client samples reported the recent use of cocaine. Stephans and Weppner[19] found that 25% of their methadone treatment sample reported that they used cocaine regularly. TRISEP data indicate an increase of 16% over the Taylor study and 10% over the Stephans and Weppner study, with 35% of the client sample reporting that they had used cocaine at least once in the week prior to the first interview (Table 2).

As the table indicates, the majority of clients use no cocaine; and, of those who use, 52% report that they used cocaine only once or twice. Table 2 also shows the distribution of use for the sample of narcotics users not in treatment. While methadone clients report

TABLE 2: Patterns of cocaine use for methadone clients and narcotics users not in treatment in the week prior to being interviewed

Cocaine Use	Methadone Clients	Narcotics Users Not In Treatment
None	64% (234)	36% (51)
1-2 times	18% (67)	28% (40)
3-6 times	10% (37)	20% (28)
7 or more times	7% (24)	14% (20)
NA, DK	2% (6)	2% (3)
	100% (368)	100% (142)

Chi square= 33.9

df=4

p=.001

cocaine use more frequently than that reported by the general population [approximately 3% of the New York State survey respondents indicated cocaine use in the prior one month period[12]], they still report significantly *less* cocaine use than narcotics users who are not currently in treatment.

TRISEP clients who report use are somewhat younger than non-users, though the difference is not significant. Unlike earlier findings that males are more likely than females to use cocaine[18], we find that cocaine has become equally attractive to women as to men in the 1980s. As earlier studies indicated, non-white clients are still significantly more likely to use cocaine than white clients.

Relationship Between Use and Crime

There are two parts to the question of whether cocaine use is associated with crime. First, is there a relationship between *any* use of cocaine and criminal activity? This question is particularly relevant in a population such as this whose income level is low and rate of unemployment high; over half the TRISEP client sample are currently unemployed. Secondly, is there a threshold effect of the amount of cocaine use and the incidence of crime; that is, beyond a particular frequency of use, is the user more likely to be involved in criminal activity?

Methadone clients who report current use of cocaine also have significantly higher levels of current criminal activity than clients reporting no cocaine use (Table 3). Of those reporting no use, only 25% report committing any property crimes and 23% any drug dealing crimes, compared to 45% of the users reporting property crime and 42% drug dealing. This relationship remains significant whether the clients are employed or unemployed, though 85% of those clients who report both the heaviest cocaine use and the heaviest involvement in crime are currently unemployed. The use of cocaine is also related to the likelihood that a client has been arrested within the last two years (Chi square = 19.96, p = .005), another indication of criminal activity among users.

Cocaine using clients are more likely to be involved in particular types of crimes (Table 4) than those who are not using cocaine— con games, forgery, prostitution, dealing stolen merchandise and stealing. For example, of the seven clients who reported committing a robbery in the prior two week period, five reported that they had also used cocaine that week, and four of those five reported using it

TABLE 3: Criminal activity in the two week prior to interview by
          cocaine use in the week prior to interview of methadone
          clients

	No Cocaine Use	Cocaine Use	Total
Property Crimes			
None	75% (180)	54% (70)	68% (250)
1-4 times	12% (29)	26% (33)	17% (62)
5 or more times	13% (31)	20% (25)	15% (56)
N=	240	128	368

Chi square= 15.84
df=2   p=.001

Drug Dealing Crimes			
None	78% (186)	58% (74)	71% (260)
1-4 times	19% (45)	34% (43)	24% (88)
5 or more times	4% (9)	9% (11)	5% (20)
N=	240	128	368

Chi Square = 13.63
df=2   p=.001

three or more times.[c] Cocaine users are also among the most active
drug dealers in the methadone client population. Thirty percent of
those clients who deal drugs more than three or four times a week
report the use of cocaine.

However, these figures are somewhat misleading. A substantial
portion (52%) of clients who report cocaine use used it only once or
twice; and, of these less frequent users, only a third report
involvement in any property crime and only 31% in any drug
dealing crimes in the two week prior period. Even though this group
of low frequency users is more active in crime than those who use
no cocaine, they are not as involved in either property or drug
dealing crimes as those using cocaine more frequently (Table 5).
The less frequent user (one who uses once or twice a week) commits
on the average one property crime and one drug dealing crime in a
two week period, compared to the cocaine user who uses three or
more times per week who is committing on the average *five* property
crimes and *two* drug dealing crimes. The difference in their criminal
involvement is significant (t = 2.96, p = .004; t = 3.65, p =

.001). With the exception of shoplifting for one's own use, this difference in criminal involvement is significant across all types of crime.

Among the group of clients who use cocaine almost daily, 46% report committing more than five property crimes and 25% report committing more than five drug dealing crimes in the prior two week period. Less than 3% of clients who use cocaine only once or twice a week are that involved in crime. To summarize, there is a significant relationship between cocaine use and crime in this population with an escalating effect with increased frequency of use. The client who uses cocaine more than a few times a week is

TABLE 4: Specific crimes committed by clients in two weeks prior to interview by their cocaine use in week prior to interview

	No cocaine used	Some cocaine used	Total	p
Shoplifting for resale				
None	94% (226)	94% (120)	94% (346)	n.s.
One or more times	6% (14)	6% (8)	6% (22)	
Shoplifting for own use				
None	88% (210)	80% (103)	85% (313)	
One or more times	12% (30)	20% (25)	15% (55)	n.s.
Burglary				
None	99% (237)	97% (124)	98% (361)	n.s.
One or more times	1% (3)	3% (4)	2% (7)	
Robbery				
None	99% (238)	96% (123)	98% (361)	
One or more times	1% (2)	4% (5)	2% (7)	n.s.
Forgery				
None	98% (235)	93% (118)	96% (353)	.02
One or more times	2% (5)	7% (10)	4% (15)	
Prostitution, pimping				
None	98% (236)	93% (119)	97% (355)	
One or more times	2% (4)	7% (9)	3% (13)	.04
Con games				
None	93% (222)	84% (108)	90% (330)	
One or more times	7% (18)	16% (20)	10% (38)	.02
Steering				
None	93% (223)	80% (102)	88% (325)	
One or more times	7% (17)	20% (26)	12% (43)	.001
Dealing stolen merchandise				
None	86% (207)	73% (93)	82% (300)	
One or more times	14% (33)	27% (35)	18% (68)	.03
N=	240	128	368	

TABLE 5: Criminal activity in two week prior period to interview
          by frequency of cocaine use by methadone clients

COCAINE USE

	1-2 times	3-6 times	7 or more	total
Property crimes				
None	67% (45)	54% (20)	21% (5)	55% (70)
1-4 times	24% (16)	24% (9)	33% (8)	26% (33)
5 or more	9% (6)	22% (8)	46% (11)	20% (25)
N=	67	37	24	128

Chi Square =13.67   df=4   p=.03

	1-2 times	3-6 times	7 or more	total
Drug dealing crimes				
None	69% (46)	57% (21)	29% (7)	58% (74)
1-4 times	28% (19)	35% (13)	46% (11)	34% (43)
5 or more	3% (2)	8% (3)	25% (6)	9% (11)
N=	67	37	24	128

Chi Square=19.96   df=4   p=.01

more likely to be involved in crime than either an abstainer or a less frequent user.

The influence of the use of other drugs with cocaine is often overlooked in the analysis of cocaine use and crime. As other investigators have pointed out, the use of cocaine alone among heavy users is uncommon[8,12,16,20] as sustained abuse often requires a counteractive depressant to alleviate what one respondent called "the cocaine crazies," or the wired, tense feeling followed by depression or a "crash" which occurs when the drug effect wears off. As one TRISEP respondent described the exhilaration/depression sequence, "It's like going up in an elevator and somebody cuts the cables."

In many cases, the involvement in crime of heavy cocaine users is in some instances linked to their involvement with an effective depressant, heroin. The use of heroin is significantly related to cocaine use in the client population (Chi square = 46.3, df = 2, p = .001). Of all cocaine users in the client population, 35% combined it with heroin. This relationship is not found between cocaine use and any of the other drugs popular among some methadone clients, such as tranquilizers, sedatives and alcohol.[21,22] Neither is the use of these other drugs related to criminal activity in this population, as are both heroin and cocaine use. Those clients who use *both* heroin and cocaine, not surprisingly, are more involved in crime than those who use cocaine alone.

It is difficult to distinguish, however, criminal activity committed to acquire heroin as opposed to that committed for cocaine. Obviously, both drugs are expensive and any combination of costs may increase the likelihood that the client will need to resort to crime. Given that increased cocaine abuse increases the likelihood that the user will need an effective depressant such as heroin to deal with ill effects, it is not uncommon to find frequent cocaine users both involved with heroin *and* more involved in criminal activity than the more occasional user.

With some notable exceptions[8,14,23] the lifestyle of the middle or lower income cocaine users has not been extensively examined. The "high roller" cocaine user who spends thousands of dollars weekly as part of a "jet set" lifestyle is often seen as representative of all users. In this sample, cocaine users hardly fit a "jet set" image. Nor are they simply heroin addicts using both heroin and cocaine in a continuation of a drug pattern established earlier. The majority of client users are working class, occasional users who, for some, when frequency of use exceeds resources, may become involved in some criminal activity. For others a low level of criminal activity may be part of their daily lives, basically unrelated to the drugs they use.[17] For still others, cocaine may be *part* of a criminal lifestyle rather than a prime motivation for it. In all of these instances, the relationship between cocaine use and crime looks empirically similar.

For example, one respondent, a forty-two year old white male, unmarried, unemployed, and a methadone treatment client reports that he used cocaine three times and heroin three or four times in the week prior to the interview and committed four property crimes and three drug dealing crimes in the prior two week period. He is actively involved in dealing a variety of stolen items in areas near his methadone program, regularly steers other users to drug suppliers for profit or acts as a drug "runner" for others. For this user, cocaine is part of a life of hustling and heroin use, a "bonus," rather than a primary motivation for criminal activity. Among his peers, his criminal activities, the ability to hustle drugs for himself and others, to "take care of business"[24] are highly regarded, and his status is high as a "righteous dope fiend".[25]

A different example is found in a twenty-eight year old Hispanic female client who uses cocaine several times a week. In a "bad week'' (meaning one in which she thinks she spent too much money on cocaine) she may spend as much as $300 on cocaine, but her typical intake is a third to a half that amount. Employed in a clerical position, she supplements her income with weekend prostitution, activities she states are carried out to cover her heavy cocaine expenses.

A final example is that of a thirty-two year old white male client in methadone treatment for twelve years, employed, and reporting the use of cocaine 3–4 times a month and occasional dealing in stolen merchandise. He is not involved in robbery or burglary for the items he sells, but rather is the middleman for others. This individual did not link his dealing stolen merchandise with his use of cocaine, but with a more general need for extra money. He was as likely to deal goods for extra money for Christmas as he was for cocaine. The criminal activity was used as a "fallback" position when finances became tight.

In the first case, the client is essentially a heroin addict in treatment using cocaine as a "bonus," as a part of a life of drug abuse. In the second example, it appears that cocaine is primarily responsible for her involvement in prostitution and cessation of use would reduce her criminal activity. The final user sees the connection between cocaine use and crime as a threshold effect, but uses his criminal activity as a supplement for many other extra expenses in addition to cocaine. All three are empirically similar, but the meaning of the drugs/crime connection is quite different.

CONCLUSION

The attractions of cocaine as a substance of abuse are well documented. It produces a short, but intense euphoria and gives the user a sense of energy and overall stimulation. For many users it is valued for providing the "rush" of heroin, without the dangers of opiate addiction.[21,26] The sense of depression which often follows heavy cocaine use, however, is a feature which encourages continued use and may precipitate the use of depressant drugs to counteract both the "crash" and the overstimulated state many users describe. Given its pleasurable effects and increased availability, it is not surprising that cocaine has become increasingly popular in all strata of society.

The relationship between cocaine and crime, however, is a

complex one. Many cocaine users use only occasionally and find that their $10–50 a month expense is manageable within the boundaries of legal sources of income. Their occasional use is also not likely to place them in a milieu of more heavy drug use and greater access to criminal opportunities. Though the occasional user is more likely to be involved in some criminal activity than those persons who use no cocaine, it is when the frequency of use exceeds the occasional level that criminal activity escalates. Prior to that point, criminal activity may serve as a safety valve for any additional expenses including cocaine, but may not necessarily be motivationally linked to cocaine use.

When frequency of use exceeds one or two times a week, the middle to lower income cocaine user is "in trouble." With limited incomes, extra expenses quickly become a problem. There is a significant escalating effect of increasing amounts of cocaine and increasing involvement in both property and drug dealing crimes— an effect attributable to both lifestyle considerations and to financial need; that is, many career addicts and/or offenders include cocaine as part of their lives, rather than as a primary motivation for their criminal careers.

Others, however, with escalating use, find that their attraction to cocaine is out of control and they require increasing amounts of money to support its use. The researchers heard many stories about individuals who had received large sums of money such as bonus checks or insurance settlements and "blew it behind coke," meaning that in a short period of time used the entire sum for cocaine. One individual described using an $1800 insurance settlement check on cocaine in the space of three days. She describes the experience as "losing control" over her own use and using and sharing it with a few others in a three day long party. This individual, a working client, would probably not have bought the quantity of cocaine used in that period without the opportunity of the settlement check presenting itself. The available money provided the opportunity for a large cocaine investment which quickly became a "run" of escalating use. Many respondents stated that heavy users do not "need" increasing amounts of cocaine to obtain the desired effect as with heroin, but *want* increasing amounts and increasing frequency to make the "run" or period of use last longer. In these circumstances, having cocaine "left over" or saving a portion for another time is reported as extremely difficult, if not impossible.

Part of the escalation of cocaine use often involves the introduction of another expensive drug, heroin. Depressants such as tranquilizers, sedatives or alcohol are reported to help balance cocaine use for a limited level of use. When cocaine use becomes heavy, a more efficient depressant is usually sought. For many cocaine users, particularly those with prior experience with heroin, heroin is used as the depressant in a "speedball combination." Since both drugs are expensive to use, the escalation of criminal activity for those resorting to crime for funds is accelerated even more rapidly. On the other hand, for those heroin addicts who are already using cocaine but whose primary drug is heroin, cocaine may not contribute greatly to their overall participation in crime. For this group, it is heroin use and the lifestyle of "taking care of business"[24] which explain their criminal activity rather than the use of cocaine.

Lifestyle versus economic motivation is a critical distinction for understanding the drugs/crime connection. Cocaine costs may encourage increased criminal activity, particularly in marginal income users, but it may both generate and be part of a lifestyle of dealing, using and criminal activity. Its weighting as a causal factor, however, is based on the resources of the user, the user's involvement and attraction to the lifestyle of cocaine use and the level of use. As with heroin, there are phases of cocaine use in which the status, recreation, excitement, etc., aspects of use predominate and phases in which the physiological and psychological compulsions (avoidance of the crash, elimination of depression, etc.) predominate. When cocaine becomes an organizing principle in the life of the user, its costs make crime almost inevitable except for the wealthy. In phases where use is more controlled and the user is less involved in the lifestyle of use, criminal activity may be minimal or non-existent. There does appear to be a threshold effect, however, beyond which both the costs and the lifestyle of cocaine predict some criminal activity.

REFERENCES

1. Gay G, Sheppard C, Inaba D, Newmeyer J. Cocaine in perspective: "Gift from the sungod" to "the rich man's drug." Drug Forum 1973; 2:409–430.
2. Mortimer WG. History of Coca. San Francisco: And/or Press, 1974.
3. Post RB. Cocaine psychosis: A continuum model. Am J of Psych. 1975; 132(3):225–231.
4. Ashley R. Cocaine: Its History, Uses and Effects. New York: St. Martin's Press, 1975.

5. Grinspoon L, Bakalar JB. Cocaine: A Drug and Its Social Evolution. New York: Basic Books, 1976.

6. Eberle EG, Gorden F. Report of the Committee on the Acquirement of Drug Habits. Am J of Pharm 1903; 75:474–485.

7. Musto D. The American Disease: The Origins of Narcotic Control. New Haven, Conn: Yale University Press, 1973.

8. Winick C. The sociology of cocaine. Proceedings of Symposium on Cocaine. New York: Division of Substance Abuse Services 1982; 62–72.

9. McLaughlin GT. Cocaine: The history and regulation of a dangerous drug. Cornell Law Review 1973; 58(3):537–572.

10. Eirsworth NA, Smith DE, Wesson D. Current perspectives on cocaine use in America. J of Psych Drugs 1972; 5(2):153–157.

11. Study ties cocaine to theft. The New York Times 1983; September 20.

12. Lipton D. Incidence and prevalence of cocaine use. Proceedings of Symposium on Cocaine. New York: Division of Substance Abuse Services 1982; 23–29.

13. Fighting cocaine's grip: Millions of users, billions of dollars. Time 1983; April 12.

14. Morningstar PJ, Chitwood DD. Cocaine user subculture. Proceedings of Symposium on Cocaine. New York: Division of Substance Abuse Services 1982; 72–88.

15. Smith DE. Diagnosis and treatment of cocaine abuse. Proceedings of Symposium on Cocaine. New York: Division of Substance Abuse Services 1982; 88–102.

16. Isbell H, White W. Clinical characteristics of addiction, Am J of Med. 1953; 14(15):558–565.

17. Hunt D, Lipton D, Spunt B. Patterns of criminal activity among methadone clients and current narcotics users not in treatment. J Dr Iss. 1984; Fall:687–702.

18. Taylor W, Chambers C, Dembo R. Cocaine abuse among methadone maintenance patients. Presented at Eastern Psychiatric Research Association. New York, November 1970.

19. Stephans RC, Weppner R. Patterns of "cheating" among methadone maintenance patients. Drug Forum 1973; 2(4):357–366.

20. Tatem AL, Seevers MH. Theories of addiction. Psych Rev 1931; 11(2):107–120.

21. Strug D, Hunt D, Lipton D, Goldsmith D. Patterns of cocaine use among methadone clients. Int J of Add. 1985; 20(8:1163-1175).

22. Hunt D, Strug D, Goldsmith D, Lipton D, Spunt B, Truitt L, Robertson K. An instant shot of "aah": Cocaine use among methadone clients. J of Psych Drugs 1984; 16(3):217–227.

23. Waldorf D. Careers in Dope. Englewood Cliffs, NJ: Prentice Hall, 1973.

24. Preble E, Casey J. "Taking care of business": The heroin user's life on the street. Int J of the Add. 1969; 4:1–24.

25. Sutter AG. The world of the righteous dope fiend. Iss in Criminol. 1966; 2:177–222.

26. Hunt D, Lipton D, Goldsmith D, Strug D. Street pharmacology: Uses of heroin and cocaine in the treatment of narcotic addiction. Dr and Al Dep. 1984; 13:375–387.

Laboratory Diagnosis of Cocaine: Intoxication and Withdrawal

Michael Lehrer, PhD
Mark S. Gold, MD

ABSTRACT. The clinical diagnosis of cocaine abuse is more difficult than previously recognized. The laboratory can play an important role in helping identify cocaine abusers and also in monitoring the progress of their recovery. An overview of the role of the laboratory is presented with the goal of optimizing the clinician's ability to apply available technology in an efficient manner. Various chromatographic and competitive binding techniques for the detection of cocaine and its metabolites in biological fluids are discussed and limits of each technique is identified. The cases of false negative and false positive results are explored and an approach to maximize benefits and economics of testing is described.

Cocaine, a naturally occurring alkaloid, is a stimulant that is obtained by extraction of the leaf of the coca bush. Some 400 years ago, the conquistadors observed that South American Indians regularly chewed wads of moistened coca leaves.

Coca leaves and cocaine are not synonymous; the latter is just one minor component of the leaf. Chemical analysis of the leaf reveals it to be rich in vitamin C, riboflavin, and thiamine; consumption of two ounces of coca leaves a day provides the poverty-stricken Indians with much of their daily vitamin requirements. In contrast, there appears to be some evidence that cocaine in the form used today depletes some of the body's store of essential neurochemicals and vitamins.[1]

Modern laboratory techniques have revealed that the size of the quid of coca leaves that can be comfortably accommodated by a

Michael Lehrer is Laboratory Director at the Psychiatric Diagnostic Labs of America, Inc., 100 Corporate Court, South Plainfield, NJ 07080 and Albert Einstein College of Medicine, Department of Laboratory Medicine, 1825 Eastchester Road, Bronx, NY 10461.
Mark S. Gold is Director of Research at Fair Oaks Hospital, Summit, NJ 07901 and Delray Beach, FL 33445.

person is such that it is unlikely that coca chewing, as practiced by the South American Indians, presents the danger that may result in the modern form of recreational use. While chewing the leaf does produce measurable levels of cocaine in human blood, these levels are extremely low.[2] The blood level of episodic cocaine users is significantly higher. Cocaine sniffing, paste smoking, rock smoking, freebase smoking and injection are the routes of cocaine self-administration.[3] One out of every 10 Americans have used cocaine at least once[4] and these people form the risk group from which the cocaine addicts and casualties are chosen.

In view of the wide-spread prevalence of drug abuse, a rational and cost effective approach to diagnosis dictates the utilization of the laboratory to rule out cocaine induced medical and psychological manifestations. Adult onset seizures, impotence, infertility, concentration and memory problems, eating disorders and other problems now have cocaine in their differential diagnosis. The laboratory also plays an important role in the treatment process. It has been demonstrated that the treatment and rehabilitation of cocaine abusers is handicapped if laboratory monitoring of drug abstention is not utilized.[5] Periodic testing is both appropriate and absolutely necessary in inpatient adolescent and drug units for a drug-free environment; it reduces the chance of drug access in hospital or treatment facility. The major reason inpatients are not outpatients is that they want and need protection from urges and access. Drug testing can help guarantee a drug-free period which makes successful treatment more likely. In these settings, tests are also indicated when the patient's motivation suddenly changes, when he asks to leave prematurely, when behavior changes or when after a suspicious pass, a patient tells of drugs on the unit or family expresses concern. Negative drug tests confirm that the patient is getting better. Positive and negative results are always useful in determining length of stay, transfer to home or to a rehab, discharge, or the patient's status and privileges. Effective use of the laboratory as a tool in the diagnosis and treatment process is enhanced by an understanding of current laboratory techniques, methodologies, and limitations.

Illicit drug use should be in the differential diagnosis of almost every patient presenting to the psychiatrist. Although most physicians agree with this concept, few take a complete history from the patient *and* family *and* follow this with a comprehensive laboratory testing for drugs of abuse, using a methodology sensitive to the low dosage, abuse dosage so common for the illicit drugs. Many clinicians focus on specific complaints or clusters of complaints, neglecting to consider the possibility of substance abuse.

CLINICAL DIAGNOSIS

The diagnosis of cocaine abuse is much more difficult than previously recognized. Physicians may encounter three clinical pictures in cocaine users: slight intoxication, overdose, and chronic cocaine use. Limited use may cause only mild intoxication. Most such patients appear giddy, energetic, and talkative and claim to feel supremely confident. Others react more adversely to low-dose cocaine and become very anxious or agitated. Physicians may note tachycardia, increased respiratory rate, pallor, and dilated pupils, which persist after the patient has "come down." Patients usually "crash" about 20–30 minutes after taking the drug and become irritable and depressed. Patients who have overdosed on cocaine present a psychiatric and/or medical emergency. Conscious patients often appear acutely psychotic or manic. They are usually paranoid, panicky, agitated or, sometimes, grandiose. They may pace around, look for unknown assailants who are "after" them, or become assaultive if they believe that they are threatened. Hallucinations of "bugs under (my) skin" ("coke bugs" or formication) or flashing lights in the peripheral vision ("snow lights") are common. Patients may pick repeatedly at their clothes or chew their lower lips to the point of ulceration. Cocaine-intoxicated patients are also potential suicide risks, particularly if they have auditory hallucinations, underlying psychiatric illness, or are chronic abusers.

Physical manifestations of cocaine overdose may be life-threatening and rapidly progressive. Neurological signs of sympathetic overstimulation, including gross tremor, facial and other muscle twitching, increased deep tendon reflexes, and a positive Babinski sign may precede grand-mal seizures or status epilepticus. Malignant hyperthermia is common due to stimulation of the heat regulatory center and increased skeletal muscle activity. Untreated patients eventually become comatose and develop a flaccid paralysis. More rarely, cocaine-induced hypertension may cause rupture of a berry aneurysm and death in predisposed patients.

Cardiovascular and respiratory collapse are ultimately the cause of death in cocaine toxicity. Tachycardia and multiple premature ventricular contractions (PVC's) occur prior to full-blown acute left heart failure and pulmonary edema. Cheynes-Stokes respirations may precede respiratory arrest. Death is usually due either to ventricular fibrillation or direct toxic effects on the myocardium.

ASSOCIATED SYMPTOMS

Chronic cocaine abusers seek treatment for numerous physical and psychiatric complaints, but do not give a history of drug use. Callers go to internists, general and family physicians, complaining of general physical problems, anergia, weakness, insomnia, sore throat, nasal sores, epistaxis, sinus problems, headaches, colds, allergies, palpitations, high blood pressure, fever, anorexia, tremor, mid life and "nerve" problems.[5] In general, they are seeking relief through prescription of a cocaine-related problem. Rather than stop using cocaine they take a variety of vitamins and prescriptions in an attempt to continue functioning. They see most every specialist and on occasion 2 or more physicians are seen in a day.

Impaired mental and cognitive function in cocaine addicts may mislead physicians into looking for psychiatric illness.

Symptoms of psychiatric illness may be mimicked by either the drug's presence or absence during withdrawal. Drug induced aggression, anxiety, depression, mania, and psychosis can apparently be produced in anyone given an adequate dose of cocaine. These and other drug induced conditions have different prognosis and must be treated differently than conditions stemming from endogenous anatomical or neurochemical aberrations. Cocaine users rarely admit use to make diagnosis easy for the physician. Physicians need to consider the possibility of cocaine use and should test for the presence of cocaine and cocaine metabolites, along with other appropriate tests, in the differential diagnosis process. It is the objective of this chapter to elucidate the role of the laboratory in the diagnosis and treatment of cocaine abuse.

METABOLISM

Cocaine is rapidly and extensively metabolized. Studies with ^{3}H labelled cocaine have demonstrated that the drug is biotransformed to ten metabolites in the rat. The concentration of unchanged cocaine in the urine is less than 10% of its major metabolite benzoylecgonine.[6] Wallace et al.,[7] demonstrated that benzoylecgonine is the principle cocaine metabolite in man with unchanged cocaine present at only substantially lower concentrations. Ambre et al.,[8] recently identified ecgonine methyl ester as an additional major metabolite of cocaine. Other cocaine metabolites, such as ecgonine and norecgonine have also been found in humans, but their trace levels in urine makes analysis of these compounds useless in diagnosis of cocaine abuse.

LABORATORY DIAGNOSIS

Laboratory methods focusing on detection of parent cocaine molecule exclusively will yield unacceptably high level of false negative results because of rapid and extensive biotransformation. Most current methodologies focus on analytical procedures capable of specifically detecting the parent cocaine molecule, as well as the benzoylecgonine metabolite, with the latter being the more important marker.

The difficulties of analyzing benzoylecgonine are well documented. This polar, amphoteric, and highly hydrophilic compound resists efficient extraction by commonly used organic solvents, ion exchange resins, or styrene-divinylbenzene copolymers (i.e., XAD-2). Separation by gas chromatography (GLC) requires derivatization of the molecule,[8] and single detection reagents commonly employed in thin-layer chromatography (TLC) do not provide sufficient sensitivity.[9] The difficulty of benzoylecgonine detection was highlighted by the results of the 1974 Center for Disease Control (CDC) proficiency testing survey where 75% of the participating labs reported false negative results on a urine specimen containing 4 ug/ml of the cocaine metabolite.[10] Only one in four participating labs correctly identified the cocaine metabolite despite its relatively high concentration level.

Since the study, various chromatographic and immunoassay methods have been developed which permit sensitive and accurate determination of benzoylecgonine. These methods are suitable for routine processing of urine samples provided that qualified and well-trained personnel are utilized and that these analytical techniques are not compromised by short cuts geared to reducing labor and material costs. Such practices negate the accuracy and specificity of these procedures. Unfortunately, such practices are all too common and it is ironic that the significant technological advances of the past decade are often negated by short-sighted economic considerations that foster false illusions of cost effectiveness. It is ironic that a decade after the 1974 CDC study, the performance of laboratories screening for cocaine abuse continues to be an issue.

A newer CDC survey, reported by Hansen et al.,[11] in 1985 clearly illustrates the scope of the problem. That survey monitored the performance of 13 laboratories serving 262 methadone treatment facilities via their analysis of spiked urine samples. It is notable that 91% of the labs had unacceptable false negative results for cocaine and its' benzoylecgonine metabolite. Only 1 out of the 13 labs surveyed performed satisfactorily in accurately detecting cocaine abuse.

In view of the variety of accurate laboratory methods that have been developed, the 1985 CDC publication concludes that

> less sensitive testing (which means that more of the drugs will be missed) may result from methodological design, personnel problems, or the reimbursement process. Because contracts are generally awarded to the lowest bidder . . . inadequate reimbursement for services may induce the need for a higher throughput of patient samples.

The study suggest that "if realistic fee schedules were established for drug testing . . . more reliable procedures would be established and better-trained personnel would be hired, leading to higher quality testing."

The results of this study clearly refute the commonly encountered fallacy that all laboratories performing drug abuse testing (and their analytical procedures) are identical. To many clinicians in the field these data are not surprising. They can recall case after case of patients admitting drug use, giving urine samples which were found negative by a laboratory. Many physicians and administrators responsible for contracting laboratory services make the assumption that all drug abuse testing methods are identical and focus on the cost of testing as the main variable. Often, the testing contract is awarded to the laboratory featuring the lowest prices independent of the laboratory's quality and reliability. Unfortunately, the widespread prevalence of this type of purchasing

approach to substance abuse testing threatens to undermine confidence in all laboratory testing results.[12]
It should be remembered that laboratory testing represents a very efficient, rapid, and cost effective way to detect and identify drug abusers. Drug testing also plays an important role in rehabilitation. Experts in drug abuse treatment consistently identify laboratory verification of a drug-free status as an indispensable tool in a successful treatment protocol.[1] However, misguided economic considerations are common causes of under-reporting of drugs, and missed chances for accurate diagnosis or treatment. This may threaten a very cost-effective and efficient system for diagnosis and treatment. The cost-conscious DRG environment of the past few years has so accelerated this trend that it threatens to subvert the primary objective of identifying drug abusers in a reliable and consistent manner.

A rational approach dictates that physicians and other purchasers of laboratory services display a healthy dose of skepticism when a laboratory markets a drug screen that purportedly is reliable and accurate in detecting some 60–70 drugs and costs only $15. Otherwise the occurrence of false negative results is not only possible but likely as the 1985 CDC study indicates. Drug ingestion or withdrawal results in the manifestations of psychosis, mania, depression, or a variety of other serious organic conditions. A false negative cocaine test can result in lengthy hospital admission that is costly and that fails to address or alleviate the patient's problems. From the point of view of cost-effectiveness, the bargain $15 laboratory drug screen can result in the waste of thousands of dollars in irrelevant medical treatment. Finally, ordering a test which is useless because it is mostly negative is truly a waste of money. Cost-effectiveness in the health care delivery system requires a broad perspective where the focus is on the total package. Such an approach would avoid the penny-wise/pound-foolish trap that is frequently seen in current laboratory contracting practices.

ANALYTICAL METHODOLOGIES

Analytical methodologies for measurement of cocaine and its benzoylecgonine metabolite can be divided into two broad categories: (1) competitive binding assays, and (2) chromatographic assays. Radioimmunoassays (RIA) and enzyme immunoassays (EIA) are examples of the former while thin layer chromatography (TLC), gas liquid chromatography (GLC), high pressure liquid chromatography (HPLC), and combined gas chromatography-mass spectrometry (GC-MS) are examples of chromatographic techniques. Each of these methodologies has a unique role and no single technique is appropriate for all analytical applications. The educated physician can make decisions about testing which can maximize the chances of an accurate diagnosis by controlling collection, choice of methodology, and selections of body fluid to be tested. A good toxicology laboratory should have the capability to perform all procedures and have the necessary instrumentation available so that appropriate "technical horse-power" can be matched to analytical needs in a cost effective manner.

Competitive Binding Assays

The various competitive binding assays operate on the principle of antigen-antibody interactions. The drugs of interest are chemically linked to larger molecules and then injected into sheep or rabbits to produce specific antibodies. An immunoassay is only as good as the specific antibody it employs; the specificity of an antibody can vary from one preparation to the next. The immunological methods used in the laboratory employ these antibodies against a specific drug (e.g., benzoylecgonine). Tagged drug molecules labelled by radioactive or enzymatic moieties, are added. The assays foster competition between tagged drug molecules, and the unknown drug for the limited binding sites on the antibody. The greater the special drug concentration in the specimen, the greater number of the tagged drug molecules that remain unbound. This free-to-bound ratio is used to quantify the amount of drug in the specimen. When the label is a radioactive moiety (e.g., ^{125}Iodine), the assay is known as radioimmunoassay (RIA). When the tag is an enzyme, the assay is known as an enzyme immunoassay (EIA).

Radioimmunoassay (RIA)

An RIA procedure for benzoylecgonine was first commercialized by Roche Diagnostics. The benzoylecgonine in a specimen being analyzed competes with the limited ^{125}I-benzoylecgonine antigen for the binding sites on the antibody. The resulting antibody complexes are precipitated and removed. The amount of unreacted ^{125}I-antigen remaining in solution is then measured in a gamma scintillation counter. The greater the amount of benzoylecgonine the more unreacted ^{125}I-antigen will remain in solution resulting in a higher count. The counting rate (counts per minute) is directly proportional to the benzoylecgonine in the specimen. The Roche RIA procedure is very sensitive and is capable of detecting benzoylecgonine at the low nanogram levels. It should be noted that the method is designed for urine samples and the manufacturer does not recommend the testing of serum.

RIA and EIA methodologies are dependent on specificity and sensitivity. This is determined by the animal generated antibodies to a given drug compound. Compounds whose chemical structures are similar to the drug of interest, often cross react with the antibodies. This cross reactivity phenomenon is important to understand because it can result in false positives or falsely elevated results. For this reason competitive binding assays are deemed to have much lower specificity compared to chromatographic techniques such as GLC and GC-MS. In the Roche RIA procedure, cross reactivity is commonly encountered with tropane alkaloids, as well as with thioridazine.[13] While cross reactivity with the tropane alkaloids is not a problem (the only probable source in humans is from cocaine metabolism), it is a potential source of false positives in the case of thioridazine, a commonly prescribed phenothiazine.

Enzyme Immunoassay (EIA)

Non-radioactive immunoassays are newer and have the advantage of avoiding hazards associated with handling radioactivity. They can also offer additional technical advantages, such as enhanced ability of automations, faster analysis time, and lower costs for small batches. On the other hand, RIA is more sensitive than EIA and thus is more efficient in detecting lower urinary drug levels. Antibodies employed for immunoassays have two important characteristics: avidity and specificity. Polyclonal antibodies contain a large number of molecular species, each with its own avidity and specificity. Monoclonal antibodies, which are produced by special cell-fusion techniques, consist of a single molecular species. Because polyclonal antibodies contain at least some highly avid molecules, they enchance the sensitivity of the assay at a cost of somewhat decreased specificity. Monoclonal antibodies enhance the specificity of the assay at a cost of somewhat decreased sensitivity. Regardless of the type of antibody used, EIA methods are susceptible to cross reactivity just as RIA methodologies.

The Enzyme Multipled Immunoassay Technique (EMIT, trademark of SYVA Co.) is the most widely used EIA methodology for benzoylecgonine. As can be anticipated, the assay cross reacts with other cocaine metabolites. In this instance, cross reactivity is not a problem because all of these components are associated with cocaine ingestion. The EMIT benzoylecgonine assay utilizes the enzyme glucose-6-phosphate dehydrogenase (G-6-PDH) as the active tag. The assay is based on the catalytic reduction of NAD to NADH which is measured spectrophotometrically at 340 nanometers. The EMIT cocaine procedure is less sensitive than the RIA assay. It is capable of detecting benzoylecgonine at a cut-off level of 300 ng/ml. Although many laboratories perform the EMIT assay, there are qualitative differences in accuracy resulting from the type of instrumentation utilized. Sophisticated automated instruments generally produce more accurate and reproducible results. Laboratories using simple manual spectrophotometers are more susceptible to instrumental and operator induced errors. As with RIA, any positive cocaine result should be confirmed by an alternate method, especially if legal considerations, employment, or clinical treatment are involved. A chromatographic methodology, such as GC-MS, should be utilized to confirm positive cocaine results obtained by either EIA or RIA.

As with RIA, the EMIT assay for cocaine is designed to be used only on urine samples. The ability to analyze serum drug levels is important because blood levels are better indicators of recent abuse than urine levels. More importantly, blood levels can often be correlated with level of intoxication and pharmacological effects. Chromatographic methods, such as GC-MS, GLC, or HPLC are suitable for the detention and quantification of cocaine and its metabolites in blood, as well as urine.

Biological Sample Extraction

An important feature of both RIA and EIA methodologies is that they do not require pretreatment of the biological sample. Chromatographic techniques generally require a sample clean-up step prior to the analysis. This is accomplished by mixing the biological sample with organic solvents to effect drug extraction at specific hydrogen ion concentrations (pH). The pH is used to optimize the aqueous-organic partition process so that drugs of interest are selectively extracted into the organic phase. Potentially interfering constituents remain in the aqueous phase which is then discarded. The organic layer containing the drugs is evaporated and analyzed chromatographically. An important benefit of the clean-up extraction step is that it serves to concentrate drug levels, greatly enhancing sensitivity of chromatographic assays. Quantification of drugs at the low nanogram level is thus frequently attainable by chromatographic techniques.

Thin-Layer Chromatography (TLC)

TLC has been used traditionally for broad spectrum screening of abused drugs. This is a fast and inexpensive method since it does not require sophisticated instrumentation. However, one must remember that the results obtained are merely qualitative, giving either a "positive" or "negative" result. Positive results cannot be quantified. It should also be noted that TLC is by far the least sensitive among the methodologies discussed in this chapter. Typically, the minimum amount of drug or metabolite necessary to yield a "positive" result falls in the 1000–2000 ng/ml range. Thus, negative TLC results may not be negative by more sensitive analytical methods. A negative TLC result may simply mean that the level of sensitivity of the method is insufficient to detect the drug in that sample. In the case of cocaine, significant drug abuse can occur at levels that would be negative when these patients are monitored by TLC. The fact that this is an all too common occurrence is evident by the 1985 CDC report.[11]

In addition to low sensitivity, TLC suffers from poor specificity. TLC relies on a reproducible migration pattern by the drug on a thin layer of absorbent (e.g., silica coated glass plate). Characterization of a particular drug is achieved by color reactions produced by spraying the plate with color complexing reagents. Coeluting biological components in the sample often interfere and may yield false positive results. If cocaine or its metabolite is present in the sample (in concentrations high enough to detect by TLC), it will be identified by the distance it migrates on the plate, and by characteristic color reaction upon spraying with appropriate chemicals. The migration and color reactions of the unknown sample are compared to known standards that are co-chromatographed with unknowns. If the unknown and cocaine standard's migration and color characteristics are similar, then the sample is deemed to be positive for cocaine.

Cocaine's benzoylecgonine metabolite can be detected by TLC in urine for 12–24 hours after ingestion of a sizable dose. This brief time frame of detectibility is another shortcoming of TLC. A cocaine abuser can ingest cocaine Saturday night, be tested Monday morning, and get a clean bill of health. Other methodologies extend the "time window" by their greater sensitivity and specificity. Thus EIA can generally detect cocaine abuse for up to a 48 hour time period, RIA for a 3–4 day time period, and GC-MS can frequently identify cocaine abuse for up to 7 days after ingestion.[14,15] Although drug analysis should be performed on urine, as well as serum samples, TLC can be only used to test urine samples. Thus, TLC shares the limitations of RIA and EIA in that it is designed to be used only for urine analyses. The ability to analyze serum drug level is important because blood level is a better indicator of recent use and more importantly, blood level correlates better with the levels of intoxication and other pharmacological or behavioral effects.

We already have discussed the problem of false negatives due to low sensitivity of TLC in detecting cocaine and its benzoylecgonine metabolite. Another complication arises from the fact that TLC is designed to screen scores of drugs simultaneously. Depending on the laboratory, "toxicology screens" are designed to detect some 30–80 drugs and metabolites in each sample simultaneously. Many additional endogenous and exogenous substances in urine may "interfere" and generate spots that can be misinterpreted and identified as a positive result. These difficulties, combined with the fact that multiple samples and standards are analyzed simultaneously, result in a complex matrix of spots and colors on the TLC plate. Interpretation and identification is performed by visual inspection and it is not difficult to either miss a drug or incorrectly identify an unrelated spot. A significant problem is the large interpersonnel variations in skills among individual technologists who perform the analyses and interpretations. Expertise and experience in TLC analysis can vary tremendously among individuals; this will have a strong bearing on the degree and extent of false negative or positive results. What to one person may appear as a transient faint yellow coloration may not be seen at all by another individual.

To assure a reasonable level of accuracy by TLC, one needs experienced and well qualified personnel. The workload must be reasonable. The technologists need to have enough time so that they can critically examine the results and investigate deviations or inconsistencies. In addition, sound laboratory protocols must be followed to optimize the analyses. This requires limiting drugs to a reasonable number so the screen is not overwhelmed. Appropriate standards for all drugs are required, as well as frequent change of visualization chemicals/developing solvents.

The results of the 1985 CDC publication[11] for cocaine, as well as for other drugs, clearly indicates that conditions necessary to optimize TLC analyses are not standard protocol in most laboratories. Low reimbursement rates for the tests frequently result in use of the inexpensive TLC procedure. Economic reality is that major improvements in quality and accuracy will be difficult to achieve as long as unrealistic reimbursement rates prevail. However, even when performed optimally, TLC analyses are in most cases not sufficiently sensitive for the differential diagnosis of cocaine induced toxic psychosis mimicking depression, mania, or schizophrenia.

GLC, HPLC and GC-MS

All chromatographic techniques can be viewed as analytical methods for the separation of mixtures into their individual components. GLC is one of the most versatile instrumental techniques for performing such separations; it is esteemed for its sensitivity, specificity, and speed of analysis. Typical analysis time ranges from 3 to 20 minutes for a sample that may contain many compounds. Recent development of capillary columns has literally enabled chromatographers to separate hundreds of compounds in a single analysis routinely. No other instrumental technique is close to having this kind of rapid analysis capability particularly for separation of complex mixtures.

All GLC consist of the following basic components: a carrier gas supply, a sample introduction inlet, a column in a temperature controlled oven, a detector, a recorder, and the electronics necessary for control. In operation, the inlet vaporizes the sample and it is then propelled through the column by the carrier gas. Separation of the mixture into its components occurs in the column, which is the heart of the GLC. The eluting components pass through the detector where they are sensed by generating electronic signals. The detector response is proportional to the amount of substance present in the sample. Identical compounds travel through the column at the same speed since their interaction with the column packing is identical. The time from injection until observed response at the recorder is referred to as retention time. A compound is identified by its unique and reproducible retention time.

HPLC is similar to GLC. A major difference in the methodologies is the use of liquid rather than gas to propel the components through the column in HPLC. Some drug classes chromatograph more optimally on HPLC (e.g., tricyclic antidepressants and benzodiazepines) while other compounds are more optimally separated by GLC. Although HPLC and GLC are similar in many respects, they are complimentary in nature and state of the art toxicology laboratories utilize both techniques extensively.

It should be noted that all chromatographic methods need to be verified to insure that retention times are accurate and that no other components in the biological sample interfere with those retention times. While GLC and HPLC represent a major enhancement in sensitivity and specificity compared to EIA and RIA, identification of components is till not absolute. The ultimate specificity available is achieved by the mass spectrometer. The mass spectrometer serves as a specific GLC detector in a technique known as combined gas chromatography-mass spectrometry (GC-MS). This technique is unique in its ability to provide absolute identification of a chemical substance.

A mass spectrometer bombards the sample with high energy electrons which results in extensive fragmentation. These fragmented ions are then detected according to their mass. Records of GC-MS analysis of substances are a unique "finger print" of the substance. No two compounds have the same fragmentation pattern. Modern GC-MS systems contain extensive computer libraries listing the fragmentation patterns of thousands of compounds. In analysis of unknown samples the fragmentation pattern is computer matched for absolute positive identification. In mass spectrometry, the samples entering the instruments must be pure. This is achieved by the use of a GLC to separate the mixture into its components and introduce them into the mass spectrometer one at a time. It is the combination of separation power of GLC and the specificity of the mass spectrometer that make combined GC-MS the most powerful analytical technique available for identification of compounds.

With reference to cocaine detection, GLC offers significant advantages over EIA methodologies in terms of sensitivity and specificity. The greater specificity is achieved because GLC identifies individual constituents. Thus the parent cocaine molecule, its benzoylecgonine metabolite, or any other metabolite or potentially interferring component can be selectively resolved. The problems of cross reactivity do not arise in GLC. With specialized detectors GLC can detect and quantify cocaine and its metabolites at the low nanogram levels. Furthermore, all biological fluids including serum can be analyzed by GLC. Combined GC-MS offers all the advantages of GLC in addition to the greatest specificity available by positive "finger print" identification.

TESTING PROTOCOL

A technically sensible and cost efficient approach to drug analysis (including cocaine) requires the availability and utilization of both competitive binding assays and chromatographic methodologies in a complimentary manner. Routine urine analyses can be automated and performed via EIA in a rapid cost effective manner. Positive cocaine results by EIA should be confirmed by GC or GC-MS. Such an approach insures against false positives. This approach is cost effective because GC-MS is utilized only for positive samples. The additional cost of GC-MS is also justified in circumstances that require additional sensitivity or specificity. GC-MS can often detect the presence of cocaine metabolites a week after ingestion, whereas EIA methodologies generally have a two day detection "window." This is an important feature if a clinician needs to rule out the possibility of cocaine use, or if sampling of a cocaine abuser cannot be performed shortly after suspected drug abuse.

GC-MS, GLC, and HPLC methodologies can be applied effectively to the testing of all biological fluids including serum. Blood levels of cocaine are important in some cases because only blood levels can be interpreted to levels of intoxication. The need to establish such relationships is important in any potentially legal situation. Blood levels are also better indicators of recent drug use. Blood levels may be useful for psychiatrists who need to know which drugs their patient used at the time of their mental status exam rather than which drugs the patient took in the preceeding week.

GC-MS confirmation of any positive cocaine result is essential in any potentially legal situation on both serum and urine samples. This is necessary because GC-MS confirmations are conclusive evidence of drug use accepted in a court of law. The use of GC-MS confirmation for situations with possible legal consequences frequently eliminates the threat of litigation because attorneys and experts recognize GC-MS evidence as ultimate proof. Situations that may have potential for legal ramifications include termination of employment or a decision not to hire or promote an individual because of suspected drug use.

SCREENING

As cocaine's abuse escalated especially in the middle and upper middle class populations,[4] more attention was directed to the acute psych-toxic effects of cocaine. Some of the symptoms present themselves as psychosis, mania, or extreme paranoia. Cocaine intoxication is indistinguishable from many classical DSM III psychiatric disorders.[15] However, acute intoxication, intermittent and regular use are difficult to diagnose. Some clues of common end stage complaints include insomnia, fatigue, headaches, depression, anxiety, irritability, poor family, poor financial status, and poor social functioning occur in the majority of regular users. Other signs and symptoms include nasal sores, epistaxis, hoarseness, chronic cough, paranoia, concentration and memory problems. Impotence or decreased libido occur in approximately 50% of regular users while seizures are less common. Urine testing is indicated in the evaluation of adolescent or adult onset of seizures because cocaine may trigger such seizures. Accidents, thoughts of suicide, suicide attempts, bankruptcy, separation and divorce commonly occur in cocaine abusers. Such complaints therefore should provide a basis for ordering urine or blood tests.

At least 20% of northeastern adolescents will try cocaine before high school graduation.[4] Cocaine use in this age group and on college campuses is increasing at an alarming rate. Commonplace in this group are sleep, mood problems, financial problems, numerous medical problems, dissociation from family and structured school activities, change of friends, declining school performance, unexplained losses of money and possessions around the home. Early detection necessitates a high level of clinician suspicion and the ability to reliably test blood or urine samples for possible drug abuse. Cocaine users have often been found to abuse a wide variety of other drugs as well. It is, therefore, important to utilize specific and sensitive drug screening techniques in both the diagnostic and treatment process. A reliable laboratory offering a full spectrum of drug abuse tests, enables clinicians to make positive substance abuse diagnosis which otherwise would be missed. If suspicion of drug use is strong, physicians should inquire about more sensitive screening procedure such as immunoassays, GC and ultimately GC-MS. Further information should be acquired about the best biofluid for the test and the best time of collection for optimum detection of the suspected drug. As a general rule, collect a morning first void urine sample, supervise the collection, and specify that the laboratory perform a specific gravity measurement on the urine sample. To insure proper detection draw a blood sample and hold. If the urine is negative and clinical suspicion remains high, test the blood. At all times be persistent and search for and call relatives for information and try to retrieve drug(s) and paraphernalia used. These can be tested as well.

The laboratory techniques discussed in this chapter apply to most drugs, as well as to cocaine. It is important that throughout the course of treatment, the drug abuser's urine is tested at least two or three times a week for cocaine and other drugs that are commonly misused (e.g., opiates, barbiturates, amphetamines, benzodiazepines, and marijuana). Testing is a valuable aid to treatment helping to promote patients' self-control and monitor the progress.[1] In general, patients are relieved to find that urine testing is a mandatory part of the treatment and recognize its value in deterring drug use. Urine testing helps to identify patients who are either unable or unwilling to stop using cocaine and those who switch to other drugs. Thus treatment is based on solid evidence provided by the laboratory.

When drug or cocaine abuse is suspected the following procedure should be followed: after a complete personal and family history, physical examination, neurological and endocrinological examination, a prescription and drug abuse inventory should be given by the physician to the patient, *and* a close relative and/or a roommate. Then a supervised urine must be obtained along with other laboratory tests which are medically indicated to properly evaluate the patient and his complaint. When used in diagnosis of drug abuse, laboratory testing has a very high yield of important, otherwise unobtainable information. This information may be life saving and may alter the diagnosis and treatment proposed. When physicians are reluctant to test for substance abuse, further deterioration of the patient may result. Early testing can reduce the damage and improve the speed and probability of successful treatment.

Urine drug analysis of suspected intoxicated drivers who pass a breathalyzer, pre-employment testing, junior and senior high school testing, and college athletics testing, have been proposed and implemented in some cases. If proper collection and chain-of-custody techniques and forensic quality methods are employed in the testing procedure, results will be very accurate and give extremely important information. As with any new medical technology we must be sensitive to all legal and ethical issues and resist the temptation to rely too heavily on testing and minimize the importance of prevention/re-education/treatment.

REFERENCES

1. Gold MS, Dackis CA. New insights and treatment: Opiate withdrawal and cocaine addiction. Clin Ther, 1984; 7, 1:6–21.
2. Holmstedt B, Lindren JE, River L, Plowman T. Cocaine in blood of coca chewers. J Ethnopharmacology. 1979; 1:69–78.
3. Gold MS, Dackis CA, Pottash ALC, Extein I, Washton A: Cocaine Update: From Bench to Bedside. In Stimmel B, (ed), Advances in Alcohol and Substance Abuse, New York, Haworth Press 5(1/2): 35–60, 1986.
4. Gold MS. 800-COCAINE. New York: Bantam Books, 1984.
5. Gold MS, Washton AM: Cocaine Abuse: Neurochemistry, Phenomenology, and Treatment. Natl Inst Drug Abuse Res Monogr Ser, 1985; 61:130–150.
6. Nayak, PK, Misra AL, Mulé SJ. Physiological disposition and biotransformation of ^{3}H-cocaine in acutely and chronically treated rats. J Pharm Exp Ther. 1976; 196:556–567.
7. Wallace JE, Hamilton HE, King DE, Bason DJ, Schwertner HA, Harris S. Gas-liquid chromatographic determination of cocaine and benzoylecgonine in urine. Anal Chem. 1976; 48:34–38.
8. Ambre J, Fischman M, Ruo T. Urinary excretion of ecgonine methyl ester, a major metabolite of cocaine in humans. J Anal Toxicol. 1984; 8:23–25.
9. Wallace JE, Hamilton HE, Schwertner HA, King DE, McNay JL, Blum K. Thin-layer chromatographic analysis of cocaine and benzoylecgonine in urine. J Chromat. 1985; 114:433–441.
10. Toxicology, drug abuse survey III: August 19th proficiency testing. Center for Disease Control, Atlanta, Georgia, 1974.
11. Hansen HJ, Caudill SP, Boone DJ. Crisis in drug testing—results of CDC blind study. JAMA. 1985; 25:2382–2387.
12. "The Ruckus Over Medical Testing." Fortune Magazine, August 19, 1985, pp. 57–62.
13. Mulé SJ, Jukofsky D, Kogan M, DePace A, Verebey K. Evaluation of the radioimmunoassay for benzoylecgonine in human serum. Clin Chem. 1977; 23:796–801.

14. VanDyke C, Byck R, Barash P, Jatlow P. Urinary excretion of Immunologically reactive metabolites after intranasal administration of cocaine followed by enzyme immunoassay. Clin Chem. 1977; 23:241–244.

15. Ambre J. The urinary excretion of cocaine and metabolites in humans: A kinetic analysis of published data. J Analyt Tox. 1985; 9:241–245.

16. Estroff TW, Gold MS. Medical and psychiatric complications of cocaine abuse and possible points of pharmacologic intervention. In Stimmel B, (ed), Advances in Alcohol and Substance Abuse, New York, Haworth Press 5(1/2): 61–76, 1986.

Structured Outpatient Treatment of Cocaine Abuse

Arnold M. Washton, PhD

ABSTRACT. This article describes specific clinical techniques for treating the cocaine abuser in a structured outpatient program. The advantages, limitations, and indications for such a program are discussed in addition to issues of treatment planning, relapse prevention, recovery groups, urine testing, family involvement, medication, and success rates.

INTRODUCTION

This article focuses on specific clinical issues and treatment techniques for outpatient cocaine abusers. Although much of this material is applicable to the treatment of cocaine abusers in office practice, discussed elsewhere in this volume, it is geared primarily toward the treatment of these patients in a structured outpatient program. The advantages of such a program include a more structured and intensive treatment approach and the unique benefits of participating in peer-recovery groups.

The need for an individualized treatment plan need not be compromised in a programmatic approach. It is essential that the program be flexible and tailor the treatment plan according to each patient's individual needs and circumstances. Cocaine abusers comprise a heterogeneous group of individuals with a wide range of treatment needs and thus no single treatment approach will be optimal in all cases. A patient's treatment needs will vary according to at least several important variables, including: the pattern and severity of cocaine abuse; the extent of drug-related psychosocial

Dr. Washton is Director of Addiction Research and Treatment at The Regent Hospital in New York City and at Stony Lodge Hospital in Ossining, NY. He is also Research Director of the National Cocaine Hotline, "800-COCAINE," at Fair Oaks Hospital in Summit, NJ. Mailing address: The Regent Hospital, 425 East 61st Street, New York, NY 10021.

impairment; the extent of simultaneous abuse of other drugs; and, the presence of co-existing psychiatric illness. Clinical techniques for assessment and treatment planning with cocaine abusers has been discussed in detail elsewhere.[1,2]

The material presented here is based primarily on the outpatient treatment programs at Regent and Stony Lodge Hospitals and the author's own clinical experience in treating a wide variety of cocaine-abusing patients in institutional and private settings. Additional material on this subject can be found in other publications.[3,4] The techniques, guidelines, and suggestions described in this article are not based on rigorous systematic investigations but rather on accumulating clinical experience with the many cocaine abusers who have been treated in our outpatient programs and on preliminary outcome studies[5] evaluating the programs' effectiveness.

ADVANTAGES OF OUTPATIENT TREATMENT

An outpatient program is the treatment of choice for the majority of cocaine abusers. Hospitalization is not required in most cases because cocaine use can usually be discontinued abruptly without a dramatic withdrawal syndrome and without substitute drugs or a gradual weaning process.

Outpatient treatment has numerous advantages. In addition to being much less costly, an outpatient program poses fewer obstacles to entering treatment. Outpatient treatment is more accessible and more acceptable to a large number of cocaine abusers who seek professional help. The reasons are fairly obvious: outpatient treatment is less disruptive to the patient's job and family and it is less stigmatizing than hospitalization. Some cocaine abusers categorically avoid treatment and perpetuate their addiction when no alternative to hospitalization is available. Because of its greater acceptability to patients, outpatient treatment may encourage an earlier entry into treatment and help to avoid the consequences of continuing drug use.

INDICATIONS FOR OUTPATIENT
VS. INPATIENT TREATMENT

Despite its numerous advantages, outpatient treatment is not clinically appropriate for all cocaine abusers. Some patients will require initial hospitalization. To properly select those who are appropriate for outpatient treatment, a careful screening and clinical evaluation are needed. The major clinical criteria for making this determination can be summarized as follows:

1. How severe is the cocaine abuse problem? Is the drug compulsion so extreme and uncontrollable that even initial cessation of drug use is unrealistic or highly unlikely unless the patient is in a controlled environment? Is the patient unable to attend treatment sessions reliably and free of drugs? Is the patient a heavy freebase or i.v. user consuming at least several grams of cocaine per day or even larger quantities during intensive episodic binges?
2. Is the patient physically addicted to other substances (e.g., opiates, alcohol, sedative-hypnotics) and therefore in need of a medically-supervised inpatient detoxification? A detailed drug use history with confirmation of recent use by sensitive and specific urine testing is required to make this assessment.
3. Are medical and/or psychiatric problems so severe that hospitalization is required for proper assessment and/or treatment? Is there a serious liver problem, sinus infection, systemic infection, neurologic problem, or other medical illness in need of inpatient evaluation or treatment? Is the patient suicidal, homicidal, severely depressed, manic, or psychotic?
4. Is there severe impairment of psychosocial functioning? Is the patient capable of caring for him/herself and continuing to work while undergoing outpatient treatment? Are family members or significant others available for support and assistance?
5. Has the patient already failed in outpatient treatment? Hospitalization may be required for those who are unable to achieve immediate abstinence in the early phase of outpatient treatment or those who relapse severely at a later stage of treatment.

TREATMENT GOALS

An outpatient program must require immediate and complete cessation of cocaine and all other drug use, including marijuana and alcohol. A goal of reduced or ''occasional'' cocaine use is unrealistic and dangerous for anyone who has become dependent on the drug. Attempts to curtail rather than discontinue cocaine use may be temporarily successful, but inevitably this will set the occasion for another cycle of compulsive use with additional negative consequences.

Requiring complete abstinence from all other mood-altering drugs provides the patient with the widest margin of safety from relapse. The long-range goal of treatment must be to develop a reasonably satisfying lifestyle without drugs. Many cocaine abusers resist the idea of discontinuing marijuana or alcohol, protesting that they have had no problems with these substances in the past and prefer to continue the practice of "social" or "recreational" use.

The rationale for total abstinence from all drugs is supported by the following observations: (1) While abstaining from cocaine, many patients seek substitute "highs" and become dependent on other mood-altering substances even those who have had no clearcut history of earlier problems with drugs or alcohol. (2) Drugs which are commonly combined with cocaine such as marijuana and alcohol often acquire the capacity to trigger urges for cocaine through associative conditioning. (3) The patient's willpower to resist cocaine can be significantly reduced by the well-known "disinhibiting" effects of alcohol and other drugs: even a single glass of wine or beer can render a patient more vulnerable to offers of cocaine. (4) A simultaneous dependency on other drugs/alcohol may not be fully recognized by the patient who has been taking these other substances not to get "high" but to self-medicate for the unpleasant side effects of cocaine. Attempts to use these other substances "occasionally" may reinitiate a pattern of abuse.

URINE TESTING

Frequent urine testing for all drugs of abuse is a critical and indispensable component of outpatient treatment. Throughout the entire course of treatment, a supervised urine sample should be taken at least 2–3 times per week and tested for cocaine and other commonly-abused drugs such as barbiturates, benzodiazepines, opiates, amphetamines, marijuana, and hallucinogens. Despite mutual trust between patient and clinician, urine testing is necessitated by the re-emerging denial and self-deceit that is characteristic of chemical dependency problems. It must be emphasized that the purpose of urine testing is not to catch the patient in a lie! Rather, urine testing is an extremely useful treatment tool that helps to counteract denial, promote self-control over drug impulses, and provides an objective indicator of treatment progress.

In order to maximize the clinical usefulness of urine testing, any consequences for drug-positive urines should be stipulated at the outset of treatment. Although a rare or infrequent "slip" may be expected during the course of recovery, any emerging pattern of more regular or frequent drug use should lead to a revision of the patient's treatment plan. Such revisions might include temporary suspension from a recovery group coupled with more intensive individual contact or, if needed, a mandatory period of hospitalization before returning to the outpatient program. The threat of hospitalization is oftimes an effective deterrant of continued drug use.

PHASES OF TREATMENT

Treatment in our outpatient programs is divided into three major phases, as outlined below. These phases are not rigidly separated from one another and the rate of progression from one phase to the next may vary considerably for different patients.

Phase 1: Initial Abstinence

The first 30–60 days of treatment focuses intensively on achieving immediate and total abstinence from all mood-altering drugs, including alcohol and marijuana. The initial target goal of the program is 30 consecutive days of complete abstinence. During this early treatment phase, patients are seen as frequently as needed (often 4–5 times per week) for emotional support, encouragement, and drug education. Patients are helped to structure their daily schedules so as to avoid boredom and "high-risk" situations previously associated with drugs. They are asked to get rid of any remaining drug supplies and paraphernalia before or on the first day of treatment. They are also encouraged to immediately sever relationships with drug dealers and users. Some of the most critical treatment issues that must be addressed during this initial phase include the following:

1. Resistance and Denial

Usually patients have a great deal of resistance to giving up all drug use, especially marijuana and alcohol. In addition, there is usually an unspoken or hidden desire to return to using cocaine "occasionally". Treatment may be seen by the patient as a way to acquire enough self-control to make occasional cocaine use possible again. Resistance may also be encountered regarding the need to make significant changes in lifestyle, peer group, and social contacts. There is often strong denial that the chemical dependency problem truly exists and a lack of understanding of how a greater acceptance of the problem can facilitate the recovery process. In order to counteract this denial, the clinician must: (a) take an extensive, detailed inventory of all previous drug-related problems and consequences with repeated use of this information to counter the patient's attempts to minimize their problem; (b) conduct drug education meetings for patients and family members describing the nature of chemical dependency problems and the stages of recovery; and, (c) after at least 2–3 weeks of complete abstinence, the patient should be inducted into a cocaine recovery group (discussed in more detail below) where the denial and resistance can be most effectively counteracted through contact with recovering peers. It must be recognized, however, that despite any initial success in breaking through the denial and resistance, these issues will tend to re-emerge in various forms throughout the treatment process.

2. Urges and Cravings

Patients must be helped to anticipate the occurrence of strong urges and cravings for drugs. Such cravings can occur suddenly and unexpectedly. They are often triggered by specific environmental stimuli (i.e., people, places, and things) that have been previously associated with cocaine or by certain internal feeling states such as boredom, depression, and fatigue that have been reliably followed by drug use in the past. Unless properly warned and educated, patients are likely to come to the erroneous conclusion that having a strong, unexpected drug urge means that the treatment is not working for them. This may lead to premature, impulsive termination of treatment. It is essential to apprise patients of potential drug cravings and to emphasize that cravings should be expected to occur as a normal and predictable part of the recovery process.

Another common misconception which leads to unnecessary relapse is that once a craving begins it will inevitably build in intensity until drug use becomes an inevitable outcome. It should be pointed out to the patient that cravings and urges are always temporary and tend to reach a peak of intensity within no longer than 1–2 hours in most instances. When a craving is first recognized, an immediate change in environment and activities may be helpful. Taking quick action to nullify one's access to drugs such as seeking out the company of non-using friends or family members is a useful way to thwart drug-seeking behavior. It is usually easier for patients to devise alternative action plans in advance of experiencing a drug urge rather than trying to do this while the urge is already upon them. Planning ahead and cognitively rehearsing alternative behaviors is crucial.

Another technique that can be useful is that of detaching oneself from the drug urge so as to examine the feeling from the vantage point of a dispassionate outside observer. Relaxation and other stress-reduction techniques may be also helpful. The goal in all of these interventions is to block or eliminate the impulse to satisfy the drug urge.

To help patients better understand and cope with potential drug urges, they should be taught the basic principles of conditioning as these apply to addictive behaviors. Discussions should include: the mechanics of environmental "triggers"; how deconditioning can work by reducing the strength of drug urges that are not reinforced by drug use; and, how drug-seeking behavior can be thwarted in its earliest stage before a relapse becomes inevitable. Explaining these conditioning phenomena helps to relieve some of the patient's excessive guilt and counter-productive feelings of uniqueness and shame. However, the importance of taking responsibility for one's own behavior, and especially for developing alternative action plans, must be emphasized.

Phase II: Relapse Prevention and Lifestyle Change

This phase of recovery begins after initial abstinence has been achieved and lasts for an additional six to twelve months. The patient enters a twice weekly cocaine recovery group and is also seen for individual and/or couples therapy at least once per week.

The major goals of this phase are to help patients: (a) avoid some of the most common and predictable factors that lead to relapse; and, (b) develop a reasonably comfortable and satisfying lifestyle that is free of drugs. The following is a discussion of some of the major clinical issues that are relevant to the prevention of relapse. Additional discussions of relapse prevention strategies in the treatment of addictions can be found elsewhere.[3,4,6,7]

1. Euphoric Recall

Cocaine abusers often have selective memory for the drug-induced euphoria. Although their search for euphoria has ended in dysphoria, depression, and many other drug-related problems, the user's thoughts and associations to cocaine still center primarily on the drug's euphoric effects. The negative experiences are easily forgotten or ignored. It is this selective memory ("euphoric recall") that heightens the patient's ambivalence about giving up cocaine entirely. To the extent that cocaine is still seen as pleasurable and appealing, the potential for relapse is heightened, particularly on occasions when the patient is feeling stressed or emotionally upset.

To counteract euphoric recall, the patient must be reminded repeatedly, throughout the course of treatment, of the numerous drug-related consequences that finally compelled them to seek help. The notion that the euphoria can be achieved without the "down side" of drug-induced consequences, must be counteracted whenever patients nostalgically reminisce about the cocaine "high". The clinician must take every opportunity to help the patient keep the negative associations to cocaine alive. We have seen evidence that the primary associations to cocaine have been changed from positive to negative in the form of spontaneous reports from patients who have said that resumption of cocaine use after several weeks or months of abstinence actually induced a dysphoric rather than a euphoric reaction. Perhaps as a result of participating in the treatment program, the associations to cocaine become increasingly negative for the patient in such a way that these negative associations eventually override the drug's euphoric effects.

2. Early Warning Signs and "Setups"

It is essential for patients to learn how to attend to the earliest warning signs of potential relapse so that preventive measures can be taken. It is usually impossible to stop an impending relapse once the situation has progressed to a point of "no return", so early recognition is critical. Patients who are headed for a relapse typically engage in a series of telling self-sabotaging acts and "setups" that precede impending drug use. These include such behaviors as re-initiating contact with drug-using friends, deciding to merely "pass by" some of the places formerly associated with buying or using drugs, or allowing stressful circumstances to intensify without taking appropriate action until cocaine use feels justifiable. The clinician must be able to spot potential warning signs and must alert the patient so that each instance can be examined and preventive actions can be taken.

3. Testing Control

After a period of initial abstinence, patients often want to see whether they have acquired enough strength to use cocaine in a limited way without losing control. This is usually a dangerous experiment and a clear indication of the patient's continuing denial. For some patients, the desire to test control may well apply to mood-altering substances other than cocaine. While the need to remain completely abstinent from cocaine may be fully accepted by the patient, he may nonetheless want to test control over alcohol or marijuana. As mentioned earlier, use of other drugs impedes the recovery process and may well lead to a cocaine relapse. These control issues may remain hidden and unverbalized by the patient without active prompting from the clinician. These issues cannot be ignored since the desire to test control is one of the surest and most common precipitants of relapse.

4. Abstinence Violation Effect (AVE)

The AVE, as described by Marlatt and Gordon,[6] is one of the most useful concepts in relapse prevention. The AVE refers to the predictable defeatist reaction experienced by an abstaining substance abuser after a "slip" back to drugs. The slip will usually set off a complex of intense negative feelings, including: feelings of failure; feelings that all progress up to that point has been lost; feelings of guilt, remorse, and self-loathing for having "given in to temptation"; and, feelings of helplessness and victimization. The slip is erroneously attributed by the patient to personal weakness or a personality defect. If these negative reactions are not prevented or short-circuited effectively, the likelihood that any single slip will escalate into a full-flown destructive relapse becomes greatly enhanced.

Patients must be educated about the AVE and be prepared with specific action plans to prevent its potentially devastating effects. For instance, at the very outset of treatment, both the patient and family members should be helped to accept the possibility that a "slip" could occur during the course of recovery and that such an occurrence would not be indicative of treatment failure. No recovering person can be guaranteed a lifetime of total abstinence upon entering a treatment program. Unrealistic expectations will only heighten the patient's sense of failure if any drug use should occur and will also increase the likelihood of premature dropout from treatment. While it is essential to recognize the possibility of relapse and how to minimize its destructive consequences, this should not be construed by the patient as permission to use drugs occasionally. Total abstinence is still the major treatment goal, but slips and relapses must not be allowed to nullify or derail the recovery process.

5. Lifestyle change

Recovery from cocaine requires more than maintaining abstinence: it requires global changes in lifestyle and attitude. Priorities and values must be re-aligned to provide a basic framework for long-lasting recovery. Additional issues that must be addressed include: interpersonal problems; establishing a regular schedule of exercise and recreational activities; making amends with family members and other victims of the drug problem; learning how to have fun without drugs; learning how to reduce stress without drugs; and, establishing a reliable peer-support network for long-term recovery.

Phase III. Consolidation

This phase usually begins after the first year of recovery and continues indefinitely after formal treatment has ended. Treatment during this phase may include individual therapy, participation in a "senior" recovery group, and continuing involvement in CA or other self-help group. The major goals are to consolidate therapeutic gains and lay the groundwork for long-term abstinence. Major tasks include: coping with "flare-up" periods, combating overconfidence and renewed denial; addressing issues of arrested development caused by drug use; and, achieving greater self-awareness, understanding, and self-acceptance.

COCAINE RECOVERY GROUPS

The recovery group is an invaluable component of outpatient treatment. Each recovery group in our program consists of 8–12 members, including both men and women. The group meets twice weekly and is co-facilitated by a professional therapist and a recovering counselor with several years of abstinence and supervised clinical experience. The group is part of a comprehensive treatment plan which may also include individual therapy, family therapy, and CA or other self-help group meetings.

Entry of new patients to the group requires at least 30 days of complete abstinence from all drugs and alcohol. Every patient in the group gives a urine sample immediately before or after every group session. The ground rules for group membership include the following: (1) the identity of all group members are held in strict confidence without exception; (2) no one is permitted to attend a group session while under the influence of drugs or alcohol; (3) reliable and punctual attendance at group meetings is required in order to maintain membership; and (4) any group member who offers drugs to another member is permanently expelled from the group immediately.

Each group includes patients who are in different stages of recovery ranging from those with one or two months of abstinence to those with six or more months of abstinence. This mixture allows new patients the benefit of immediate exposure to positive role models and provides them with living examples that recovery is indeed possible. It also provides the more senior members of the group with a healthy reminder of their own experiences in the early stage of recovery. The groups promote rapid identification among peers and provide a forum for education and experiential learning about a wide variety of recovery issues. The basic themes of the group are those of accepting that one has a chemical dependency problem and the ways in which one's behavior, lifestyle, and attitudes must change in order to achieve long-lasting recovery.

Group sessions often focus on specific relapse prevention techniques as these may relate to the immediate and current problems being experienced by one or more members. Many patients find that in the group sessions they are best able to resolve feelings of uniqueness, guilt, and shame. Since many are middle-class individuals with good jobs or careers and no history of previous drug addiction, the opportunity to identify readily with others like themselves seems especially important. Beyond education and role-modeling, the group serves a vital role in stimulating and maintaining the patient's motivation to remain drug free. Peer pressure and support are almost always needed to overcome the strong ambivalence about giving up drugs.

At the beginning of the program, many new patients are strongly resistant to the idea of joining a recovery group because of heightened concerns about confidentiality and the discomfort of sharing personal problems with strangers. Our experience indicates that contrary to these negative expectations, patients usually adjust rapidly to the group situation within the first few sessions and respond very positively to their newly-found peer-support network. It must be recognized, however, that some individuals are not clinically appropriate for a recovery group, including those with serious psychiatric disturbance and those who object so strongly to entering the group that such an attempt would likely have a destructive influence on the individual patient and on the group.

For patients who have achieved at least 9–12 months of abstinence, we have found that a special senior recovery group helps to keep the recovery process moving forward. At this stage of treatment, the initial recovery group begins to have diminishing usefulness to the more advanced patient. The senior group provides a forum in which longer-term recovery issues can be dealt with more effectively. The focus of group sessions will often shift from early abstinence issues to topics such as relationship problems, self-esteem problems, sexual problems, and other personal matters which can be discussed more freely when drug urges and the immediate threat of unpredictable relapse have diminished.

SELF-HELP GROUPS

Participation in a self-help group can be a valuable adjunct to outpatient treatment and can also provide a source of ongoing support for the patient after formal treatment has ended. Self-help groups such as Cocaine Anonymous (CA), Alcoholics Anonymous (AA), or Narcotics Anonymous (NA), are based on the traditional 12-step program of recovery which advocates total abstinence from all mood-altering chemicals as the best way to arrest the disease of chemical dependency. Participation in these groups should be strongly encouraged in the vast majority of cases, but need not be made an absolute requirement of outpatient treatment in every single case. Some patients need preliminary help in overcoming their initial fears and hesitations about attending self-help meetings. In general, the more severe a patient's addiction, the more likely he/she is to accept the 12-step philosophy and the need to attend self-help meetings.

FAMILY INVOLVEMENT

Close family members and especially the spouse or parents of the cocaine abuser should be involved in the treatment for a number of reasons. Family members can provide additional information about the patient's drug use and other behavior. Well-intentioned family members often function as enablers by making excuses for the cocaine abuser, providing money for the drug, or otherwise trying to spare the patient from suffering the consequences of his/her behavior. Family members need instruction and guidance in how to deal with the cocaine abuser and how to provide the necessary support to foster the patient's recovery. They also need an opportunity to deal with their own feelings of anger, blame, guilt, and victimization so as to minimize family stress and confusion which could itself lead to the patient's early relapse and treatment failure.

PHARMACOLOGIC TREATMENT

There is no conclusive evidence that antidepressants, lithium, amino acids, or other psychotropic agents block the cocaine euphoria, ameliorate post-cocaine symptoms, or eliminate craving for cocaine. There is no known cocaine antagonist and no medication that has been shown to prevent relapse, despite earlier claims which have not been replicated. If such medications were found they might indeed be helpful, especially in extreme or intractable cases where psychological interventions alone have failed. Recent inpatient trials with bromocriptine,[8] a dopamine agonist, suggest the potential use of this drug in eliminating urges and cravings for cocaine during the immediate post-drug abstinence period. We have recently initiated a preliminary trial of bromocriptine in outpatient cocaine abusers and our as yet unconfirmed observations suggest that the medication may be useful in helping patients to achieve initial abstinence from cocaine. The clinical efficacy of bromo-criptine in treating cocaine abusers remains to be determined by controlled systematic studies.

PSYCHIATRIC ISSUES

Depression is a common side effect of chronic cocaine abuse and a common complaint during initial cocaine abstinence. Symptoms mimicking bipolar disorders, attention deficit disorders, and anxiety disorders may also be generated by cocaine abuse. Therefore, it is essential to allow a sufficient post-cocaine recovery period before making a definitive psychiatric diagnosis or introducing psychotropic medication. In cases where there is a genuine dual diagnosis of psychiatric illness and chemical dependency, both problems must be treated. It is nonetheless imperative that the drug abuse problem be dealt with as a primary disorder and not merely as a symptom of the psychiatric illness. In order to avoid unrealistic or distorted expec-tations, patients who receive psychotropic medication should be informed that the medication is to treat their psychiatric disorder and not to prevent relapse to drug use. The medication cannot be a substitute for the lifestyle change and other treatment efforts that are essential to recovery.

OTHER INTERVENTIONS

In addition to formal treatment interventions, a regular schedule of exercise and planned leisure-time activities is an important feature of many patients' recovery plan. These activities help not only to reduce stress but also to instill a feeling of greater control over one's life. Workaholism and lack of satisfying social or leisure time are often precursors to relapse.

SUCCESS RATES

Success rates in an outpatient program will depend, of course, upon a variety of factors including the severity of abuse, the patient's motivation to be drug free, and the extent to which the program meets the patient's most critical treatment needs. The highest success rates can be expected in those patients who have a strong desire to stop using cocaine, a history of good functioning before cocaine, and those who are able to eventually accept the need for lifestyle change and total abstinence. In a recent study of 127 patients who entered our outpatient program, we found that over 65% of patients completed the 6–12 month program and over 75% were still drug free at 1–2 year follow-up.[5]

REFERENCES

1. Washton AM, Stone NS, Hendrickson EH. Clinical assessment of the chronic cocaine abuser. In Marlatt GA & Donovan DM (Eds.), Assessment of addictive behaviors. New York: Guilford Press, in press.
2. Kleber HD, Gawin FH. The spectrum of cocaine abuse and its treatment. Journal of Clinical Psychiatry, 1984:45, 18–23.
3. Washton AM, Gold MS, Pottash AC. Cocaine abuse: techniques of assessment, diagnosis, and treatment. Psychiatric Medicine, in press.
4. Washton AM. Treatment of cocaine abuse. Psychiatric Clinics of North America, in press.
5. Washton AM, Gold MS, Pottash AC. Success rates in cocaine abuse treatment. In LS Harris (Ed.), Problems of drug dependence, 1985. NIDA Research Monograph, Washington, DC: US Gov't Printing Office, in press. Also: paper presented at Annual Meeting of the American Psychiatric Association, Dallas, May 1985.
6. Marlatt GA, Gordon JR. Relapse prevention. New York: Guilford Press, 1985.
7. Zackon F, McAuliffe WE, Ch'ien JMN. Addict aftercare: recovery training and self-help. NIDA Treatment Research Monograph. Washington DC: US Gov't Printing Office, DHHS publication number (ADM)85-1341, 1985.
8. Dackis CA, Gold MS. Bromocriptine as a treatment for cocaine abuse. Lancet, 1985:11: 1151–1152 (letter).

Social Network Therapy for Cocaine Dependence

Marc Galanter, MD

ABSTRACT. The article describes an approach to the treatment of cocaine dependent patients in which the patient's social network is used to bolster his attempts to achieve stable abstinence. The network is drawn from persons close to the patient, typically members of his immediate family or close friends, and is used for social support in assuring compliance with the treatment regimen and in undercutting denial. The function of the regimen is explained to the patient and network members: It is conducted to assure the patient's abstinence from the outset of treatment, to mitigate against the occurrence of slips, and to support reintegration into treatment should relapses to alcohol or drug use occur.

The social network of a cocaine dependent person can be utilized as an integral part of his rehabilitation. For most such patients this resource, in addition to the relationship with an individual therapist, can serve as an effective vehicle for achieving abstinence and preventing future relapse. In this article the techniques for implementing this approach will be described and relevant case histories will be used so as to illustrate the way in which these techniques are implemented.

The utility of this approach is suggested by modalities already in use in the treatment of addiction, since social supports of various kinds underlie the principal treatments currently used in the addiction field. These modalities include the mutual support available in the fellowship of Alcoholics Anonymous as well as its residential counterparts in drug-free therapeutic communities. Social supports are essential too in modalities which rely on the strength of family ties, ones which have gained considerable popularity in recent years in the treatment of addiction, such as family therapy and multiple

Marc Galanter is a Professor of Psychiatry at Albert Einstein College of Medicine, Bronx, NY 10461.

family groups.[1,2] Both these modalities and their naturalistic counterparts demonstrate that the social cohesiveness and affiliative
bonds inherent in a network of social relations can exert a compelling influence in controlling addictive behavior.[3] The approach to
be described here will illustrate the further use of such bonds in a
manner which is readily manageable by the practitioner of individual psychotherapy as well.

Social network therapy for cocaine dependence is also of potential
value solely because of a lack of other available modalities sufficient
to establish full control over the addictive inclinations of the patient.
Thus, individual therapy in isolation has been observed to provide
limited long-term benefit for assuring abstinence in addictive illness.[4] Pharmaco-therapeutic techniques, particularly the use of tricyclic antidepressants, show promise in yielding diminished craving,[5] but have yet to be demonstrated acceptable in a wide variety
of clinical settings. Finally, self-help programs such as Cocaine
Anonymous and some ambulatory therapeutic community programs
do show promise for aiding patients in achieving abstinence,[6] but
typically demand a considerable input from the patient in the way of
time and personal commitment, one which many cocaine abusers are
reluctant to make. Altogether, therefore, the individual practitioner
is still left with the need for treatment options which will bolster his
ability to achieve therapeutic success in office practice.

In reviewing the ensuing material, the reader should focus on
those aspects of the treatment outlined here which are *at variance*
with his usual therapeutic approach, so that he may use them to
complement his own therapeutic style. It is essential for the clinician
to rely on acquired clinical judgment and experience, but it is
equally important that he be prepared to depart from his usual mode
of psychotherapeutic treatment in treating the cocaine addict by
recourse to network therapy. For example, activity rather than
passivity is essential when a problem of drug exposure is suggested;
the concept of therapist and patient enclosed in an inviolable
envelope must be modified; immediate circumstances which may
expose the patient to cocaine use must take precedence over issues
of long-term understanding and insight.

PATIENT SELECTION

Network therapy can be useful in addressing a broad range of
addictive problems, and I have described its use with the alcoholic

patient elsewhere.[7] Patients who are most suitable for treatment based on network therapy are characterized by the following clinical hallmarks of addictive illness seen with addiction to agents, as well as cocaine. First, when the cocaine dependent patient initiates consumption of the drug, he frequently cannot limit his intake to a reasonable and predictable level. (This phenomenon has been termed *loss of control* by clinicians who treat alcohol- or drug-dependent persons.) Second, the cocaine dependent person consistently demonstrates *relapse* to cocaine use; that is to say, although he may have attempted to stop using the drug, he has nonetheless returned to it, despite a specific intent to avoid such relapse.

This treatment approach is not necessary for those abusers who can, in fact, learn to set limits on their use of cocaine; such abuse may be treated as a behavioral symptom in a more traditional psycho-therapeutic fashion. Nor is social network therapy directed at those patients for whom the addictive pattern is most unmanageable, such as long-term intravenous drug users, and others with unusual destabilizing circumstances such as homelessness, severe character pathology, or psychosis. These latter patients may need special supportive care such as long-term residential treatment or additional psychotropic medication.

SETTING UP THE NETWORK

It is important that the patient be introduced to the idea that his treatment will include the involvement of persons in his immediate social network from the outset. Because drug-dependent patients are threatened by the possibility of losing access to their addictive agent when they first encounter treatment, they may deny the full scope of their problem even if they have voluntarily sought help, a significant other is essential in both history-taking and in implementing a viable treatment plan. A person close to the patient can often cut through the denial in the way that an unfamiliar therapist cannot, and can therefore be invaluable in setting a standard of realism in dealing with the addiction.

Some patients avow that they wish to master the problem on their own. This is often associated with their desire to preserve the option of continued substance abuse, and is born out of the fear that an alliance will be established independent of them, perhaps to prevent their implicit desire to continue with the drug. While a delay may be tolerated for a session or two, there should be no ambiguity at the outset. Effective treatment can only be undertaken on the basis of a therapeutic alliance around the drug issue which includes the support of significant others. It is expected that a network of close friends and/or relatives will be brought in within a session or two at the most.

The First Contact

The engagement of the patient along with a social network, particularly at the outset of treatment entails a considerable degree of flexibility in style on the part of the therapist, along with a concomitant persistence in focussing on the essential role of the network. Even the initial exchanges with the patient over the telephone should be considered in this light. Even if the patient's problem has been described beforehand by a referring party, a brief exchange at this time can yield information. The therapist will then do well to engage the cocaine dependent person in an exchange that is sufficient to address two important questions.

The first is whether the therapist can realistically plan with the patient for him to remain abstinent from cocaine until the time of their first face-to-face meeting. This is important because of a considerable attrition that takes place even before the first meeting due to the patient's denial of the need for treatment; this attrition is greatly enhanced by ongoing use of the drug. On the other hand, the patient who successfully maintains abstinence is in a better position to be realistic about the advantages to be gained through abstinence and to come to treatment as agreed; he has also begun to define a therapeutic alliance based on a commitment to relinquishing his addiction. The therapist will therefore do well to establish a plan for maintaining abstinence from the very outset, that is to say, at the time of the first telephone exchange, if this is feasible.

The second question to be resolved at the first call is whether the patient will be able to bring to the initial session a member of his social network who can aid him in achieving abstinence. The presence of such a member will considerably enhance the exchange which takes place and begin to build toward the full thrust of the network therapy. On the other hand, if the patient lacks the resources to bring in such a person, or if his uneasiness about engaging in treatment is such that he is not likely to cooperate in this fashion before the first meeting, then this issue will have to wait until then.

An experience with one patient illustrates how these questions were addressed. A 29 year-old lawyer called, and when asked about his problem, he indicated that his principal reason for coming to treatment was his difficulty with cocaine use of several years duration. A brief exchange revealed his willingness to take steps necessary to deal with his dependency, but a great difficulty in exercising control over his daily heavy use of the drug. Further questioning revealed that his wife was at home with him and that she was eager to see him address this problem. I discussed with him the feasibility of his staying away from the drug until our scheduled appointment two days later, and then asked if it would be possible to clarify this matter with his wife, too. It seemed to me that the patient would have difficulty in refraining from taking cocaine in this interim period, and therefore strategically important to initiate assistance from his wife so that the idea of her involvement early on in the treatment be introduced, and so that she could be of assistance at this juncture. The three of us together next considered their going out of town for the intervening weekend, which was not feasible, but did agree that they would spend the following night with his parents, as they felt that this would help to bolster his abstinence.

After exchanges to this effect with the patient and his wife, all in this first phone call, the understanding was reached that he would attempt to remain abstinent by means of the agreed upon plan, I acknowledged that this might be difficult, and even that if he should take some cocaine he should not become discouraged, as this was not uncommon at the outset of treatment. Furthermore, it was agreed that his wife would be supportive in his endeavor, but that whatever transpired both he and she would appear in my office at the appointed time. In matter of fact, he did succeed with her help in abstaining over the two days, an accomplishment which left him feeling positive about the upcoming therapeutic endeavor.

This exchange illustrated the give and take in the initial negotiations to establish an understanding regarding treatment, so as to define in a supportive way the nature of the therapeutic alliance.

Defining the Network's Membership

Once the patient has come for an appointment, establishing a network is a task undertaken with active collaboration of patient and therapist. The two, aided by those parties who join the network initially, must search for the right balance of members. The therapist must carefully promote the choice of appropriate network members, however, just as the platoon leader selects those who will go into combat with him. The network will be crucial in determining the balance of the therapy. This process is not without problems, and the therapist must think in a strategic fashion of the interactions which may take place among network members. The following case illustrates the nature of their task.

A 25 year-old graduate student had been abusing cocaine since high school, in part drawing in funds from his affluent family, who lived in a remote city. At two points in the process of establishing his support network, the reactions of his live-in girlfriend who worked with us from the outset were particularly important. Both he and she agreed to bring in his 19 year-old sister, a freshman at a nearby college. He then mentioned a "friend" of his, apparently a woman whom he had apparently found attractive, even though there was no history of an overt romantic involvement. The expression on his girlfriend's face suggested that she did not like this idea, although she offered no rationale for excluding this potential rival. The idea of having to rely for assistance solely on two women who might see each other as competitors, however, was unappealing. I therefore finessed the idea of the "friend," and we moved on to evaluating the patient's uncle, whom he initially preferred to exclude, despite the fact that his girlfriend thought him appropriate. It later turned out (as I had expected) that the uncle was perceived as a potentially disapproving representative of the parental generation. I encouraged the patient to accept the uncle as a network member nonetheless, so as to round out the range of relationships within the group, and did spell out my rationale for this inclusion. In matter of fact, the uncle turned out to be caring and supportive, particularly after he was helped to understand the nature of the addictive process.

THE NETWORK'S TASK

Rules of the Network

The following guidelines should be made clear from the first, so that network members can collaborate in implementing their respective roles in working with the patient. Above all, they should be conveyed by example. The correction of misapprehensions about these norms should be given a high priority; similarly, violations of these guidelines are discussed as soon as detected, and in a supportive manner.

1. *The purpose of the network* is to help the patient maintain his abstinence; unrelated benefits for other members are not pursued in network sessions, either by patient, network members, or therapist.
2. *Information relevant to the patient's abstinence* or slips into drug use will be promptly reported to the therapist and to other network members.
3. *Supportiveness* for the patient is primary. Members should help him to deal with problems he confronts regarding abstinence but not be critical of his difficulties in achieving a recovery.
4. *If a slip is detected* by a network member, he will offer the patient assistance, but will not impose a course of action without consultation with the therapist.
5. *The nature of confidentiality* is important. The patient's own exchanges with the therapist which are unrelated to drug problems are kept in confidence. Information revealed by network members to the therapist, however, will be brought up in the group if relevant.

The Therapist's Role

As conceived here, the therapist's relationship to the network is like that of a team leader, rather than that of a family therapist. The network is established to implement a straightforward task, that of aiding the therapist to sustain the patient's abstinence. It must be directed with the same clarity of purpose that an organizational task force is directed to win a game at sports, build more cars, or revise its management procedures. Competing and alternative goals must be suppressed, or at least prevented from interfering with the primary task.

The therapist must convey a certain attitude toward network members. They should not be led to expect symptom relief or self-realization. This prevents the development of competing goals for the network's meetings. It also assures the members' protection from having their own motives scrutinized, and thereby supports their continuing involvement without the threat of an assault on their psychological defenses. On the other hand, since network members have—kindly—volunteered to participate, their motives must not be impugned. Their constructive behavior should be commended. It is useful to acknowledge appreciation for the contribution they are making to the therapy. There is always a counterproductive tendency on their part to minimize the value of their contribution.

This pragmatic approach is illustrated in the way the therapist forges the network into a working group so as to provide necessary support for the patient between the initial therapy sessions. He may plan contacts between the network members at the outset of treatment; they typically include telephone calls usually made by the patient, dinner arrangements, and social encounters. The therapist should pre-plan these during the joint session for times when alcohol or drug use is likely to occur. The therapist should make clear to network members that relatively little unusual effort will be required for the long term, that after the patient is stabilized, their participation will come to little more than attendance at infrequent meetings with the patient and therapist. This is reassuring to those network members who are unable to make a major time commitment to the patient, as well as to the majority of patients who do not want to be placed in a dependent position.

The therapist himself should be available for consultation on the phone, and should indicate to the patient that he wants to be called if problems arise. This makes the therapist's commitment clear, and sets the tone for a "team effort." It begins to undercut one reason for relapse, the patient's sense that he will be on his own if he is unable to manage the situation. The astute therapist, though, will assure that he does not spend excessive time at the telephone or in emergency sessions, and therefore will develop a support network which can handle the majority of problems involved in day to day assistance to the patient. This will generally leave the therapist to respond only to occasional questions of interpreting the terms of the understanding between himself, the patient, and support network members. If there is a question about the ability of the patient and network to manage the period between the initial sessions, the first few scheduled sessions may be arranged at intervals of only one to three days.

For the long term, though, the network is established to provide consensual support for abstinence by their sharing with the patient and therapist their own observations and reactions relative to the patient's ongoing abstinence. This openness and commitment to the common task must be fostered from the outset, and the therapist's activity in promoting proper attitudes among network members is invaluable in stabilizing the mutual alliance and providing the patient necessary support for his abstinence.

The therapist's emphasis on openness as a vehicle in consolidating the network is illustrated in the following sequence of events which took place in the treatment of a 43 year-old homosexual corporate executive. It was necessary to develop a support network for this patient in the absence of any family members in the immediate area, and three close social acquaintances of the patient were chosen. These men were quite willing to cooperate with the therapist, but because they had used cocaine themselves a fair amount in their own homosexual subculture, they tended not to acknowledge the full scope of its negative impact.

On one occasion it became apparent to one of the network members that the patient himself had begun using cocaine again, and he called to inform me of the problem. At the ensuing session, however, this member was apparently reluctant to bring the matter up, even though the group was queried as to whether any events of concern had arisen since the last meeting. At long last, I had to raise the issue myself, but used it to underline the importance of immediately addressing the problems that arose when either patient or network member himself was uneasy about confronting the issue of repeated cocaine use. The network member who had called me then felt free to recount what he had observed and his concerns for the patient. The discussion that ensued between the patient and other network members helped all four parties to understand the vulnerability to denial they all had to confront, and served to integrate the steps we then took in assuring future abstinence into a helpful psychological framework.

The Frequency of Network Sessions

At the outset of therapy, it is important to see the patient with the group on a weekly basis, for at least the first month. Unstable circumstances demand more frequent contacts with the network. Sessions can be tapered off to bi-weekly and then monthly intervals after a time. In order to sustain the continuing commitment of the group, particularly that between the therapist and the network members, though, network sessions should be held every three months or so for the duration of the individual therapy. Once the patient has stabilized, the meetings tend less to address day-to-day maintenance of abstinence and more, the patient's general adaptation to a drug-free life. A typical network session begins with a recounting by the patient of any events related to his cocaine use. Reflections on the patient's progress and goals, or sometimes on relations with the network members, may then be discussed. In any case, it is essential that the understanding be supported that network members notify the therapist if they are concerned about the patient's possible use of cocaine, and that the therapist enlist the aid of the network members if he becomes concerned over a potential relapse.

Free-Standing Network Contacts

One value of the network therapy is that the group can play a useful role in providing direct support at anticipated times of difficulty *outside* the office context. It is therefore important for the therapist to work with the patient and network members to address any uncertainty he or they may feel about the patient's ability to refrain from cocaine *between* scheduled sessions. So long as there is a good working alliance within the group, this can be done rather effectively by means of open discussion. The patient himself, for example, may acknowledge that he feels compelled to call a supplier at certain times of the day or in certain settings. Other network members, too, may point out to him those times at which they think he is most likely to be vulnerable, times at which they have seen him seek out cocaine but which he may not perceive himself.

All this information is useful in planning for contacts between patients and network members between scheduled therapy sessions, when necessary. These contacts are arranged so as to take place at a time when they will abort the likelihood of drug taking before craving has moved to the point that the patient can no longer control his actions and moves to obtain cocaine. For example, one patient had regularly called one of his suppliers in the late afternoon on work days to have him deliver a supply of cocaine which he would then take upon leaving work. This impulsive behavior was one that he found difficult to control, even though he realized that it was part of a dangerous pattern, one which he hoped to change. In order to prevent relapse at such times, I arranged with him and another network member, an associate at his place of business, that they speak together in the early afternoon, and also arrange to meet immediately after work on work days until the time of the next session. This was also done at a subsequent time when, due to events in his life, the patient was particularly vulnerable to further drug taking. The intercession of personal and cognitive commitments associated with the network enabled the patient to avoid making his calls.

Another way in which free-standing network meetings can be used is to deter relapse during extended periods of time when the therapist will not be present. Thus, in the early stages of treatment one may arrange for such a meeting during the course of the week of absence, or for a meeting or two over the course of a period of several weeks that the therapist will be away. In order to assure that these meetings are held at a time when the patient may be tempted to "forget" them because of a rising desire for drug use, it is often best to plan beforehand with the network for the time and place.

Planning at a network meeting for a free-standing session may thus take place weeks before the therapist is away. In anticipation of that planning meeting the therapist and patient should themselves discuss the patient's relative vulnerability during the period of absence as well as what cues precipitate drug use in the patient.[8] It is important that the patient himself feel that an additional meeting is part of his active participation in the therapy, and not one that is imposed on him. Such meetings may therefore be held in the context of a dinner party at a restaurant which the patient hosts for the members of his network.

Confidentiality

Questions of confidentiality and the nature of the therapist's own commitment to the patient's interests over those of other network members must be considered, given the number of complex interactions inherent in the network therapy. The overriding commitment of the therapist to the patient is that he support him in maintaining the drug-free state, and in order to achieve this, open communication on matters regarding alcohol and drugs should be maintained among the network, the patient, and the therapist.

On the other hand, the therapist must set the proper tone of mutual trust and understanding so that the patient's right to privacy not otherwise be compromised. Thus, it must be made explicit that absolute confidentiality applies to all other (non-drug-related) communications between therapist and patient, and that network members should not expect to communicate with the therapist about problems facing the patient which do not directly relate to his drug abuse. The therapist also, clearly, does not intercede to address problems between network members and the patient that do not directly compromise the patient's abstinence.

The experience of one writer addicted to cocaine illustrates the delicacy which must be exercised in this matter. The patient's network consisted of his wife and one close friend, both of whom had worked closely together with him over a period of several months to help stabilize his abstinence. Exchanges had been open and free regarding the problems which he had confronted in effecting this, and on a few occasions I had consulted with the wife over the phone over our mutual concerns regarding his drug use. On one subsequent occasion, however, she called me to express her own considerable anxiety over the fact that the patient had begun to experience difficulty in his writing, and had been feeling anxious. She was concerned less about his use of drugs at this time, than about the distress which he was experiencing and his seeming loss of function.

In matter of fact, the patient himself had been discussing this issue in his individual session, but this was an issue that did not relate to an immediate vulnerability to drug use, and therefore I felt that it was inappropriate to discuss the matter with his wife, since this would compromise the autonomous nature of the individual therapy. At the same time, I did not want to put off the wife, as she herself was vital to the support network. Fortunately the woman was sensitive to this issue, and able to discuss the differences between drug-related and unrelated issues in this case, as well as the implications for the patient's confidentiality of our discussing this matter on the phone. By means of my clarification she was able to accept the distinction drawn.

Dealing with the Recurrence of Drug Use

Individual and family therapists[9] often consider the alcohol- or drug-abuser as a patient with poor prognosis. This is largely because in the context of traditional psychotherapy, there are no behavioral controls to prevent the recurrence of drug use, and resources are not available for behavioral intervention if a recurrence takes place— which it usually does. A system of impediments to the emergence of relapse, resting heavily on the actual or symbolic role of the network, must therefore be established. The therapist must also have assistance in addressing any minor episode of drug use, so that this ever-present problem does not lead to an unmanageable relapse or an unsuccessful termination of therapy.

It is important to consider here how the support network can be used to prevent recurrences of drug use, when, in fact, the patient's prior association with these same persons did not prevent him from using alcohol or drugs. To this end, it is necessary to clarify how an ongoing network may be used to abort an emerging relapse. A high index of suspicion for signs of trouble is important, as is a clear understanding with the network members that they would be mobilized when necessary. The important factor here is that an enlightened consensus is developed in collaboration with the patient while he is drug free and more objective and they themselves are cooperative.

One experience with a 34 year-old cameraman who became addicted to cocaine illustrates the way in which the network is used in dealing with relapse. The patient had acquired a considerable amount of capital, dealing in cocaine extensively, primarily among friends and acquaintances, in order to support his habit. After a point, though, his wife moved out of the house and took their baby, saying she could no longer tolerate his heavy drug use. Ironically, she had been using cocaine herself, but to a lesser extent. The couple was reunited in the context of a therapy predicated on the patient's abstinence (and secondarily, on hers too). This was supported by a network consisting of the wife, the patient's brother, and a good friend.

The issue of relapse arose in an interesting context, one which illustrates how the subtleties of attitude among network members influence the patient's behavior. Each network member played an important role. The wife, seeing her husband's boredom and disillusionment at the contraction of his successful but illicit career in drug sales, suggested that he might be able to sell cocaine, although not use it himself. His friend who had previously experienced difficulties with cocaine and had stopped on his own, but still used it occasionally, gave a mixed message by his own example. The brother, a staunch critic of any drug use (and all other human frailties, for that matter) was feared by the patient as unable to empathize with his problems, presented a forbidding figure whom he hesitated to confide in. No network member provided an ideal figure for support and commitment to abstinence.

Difficulties gradually emerged when the patient had been in treatment for six months, with only one occasion of use of a small amount of the drug. I was away on vacation for a month and returned to find that he had again taken cocaine on two occasions. On a third, he had brought some over to the home of his friend from the network, and was fortunately persuaded to return it to the supplier. Although the patient had not taken the drug on this latter occasion, it seemed essential to seize on the circumstance to reverse his orientation toward intermittent use. I therefore summoned up the network for weekly meetings, three in all, at which time the risks inherent in the patient's occasional use of drugs were examined in a non-judgmental way. The group affirmed what had seemingly been clear, but had not been fully adopted, the need for total abstinence in order to avoid the vulnerability to serious relapse. In this situation it became necessary to explore the ambivalence of the wife and the friend about the patient being abstinent. The brother's rigidity was also addressed to underline that a judgmental attitude was not helpful in this situation. Here again, the exchanges helped the patient renew his commitment to the goal of the therapy.

SPECIAL ISSUES

Reluctant Patients

Certain circumstances may justify incursions on the patient's autonomy, so as to assure compliance with treatment. This is particularly true when the patient begins treatment reluctantly, only on the basis of overt pressure from the family or employer, or when the possibility of relapse will have grave consequences. Options for intrusive measures include the possibility of financial constraints, moderating the threat of a spouse's moving out, and urine monitoring. These, of course, can only be undertaken after considerable discussion, hopefully involving the patient himself.

The use of the social network thereby provides the opportunity for intervening with patients who might otherwise be unwilling to enter into treatment, by means of "striking up a bargain," so to speak, which meets both the interests of the patient and the concerns of the members of the patient's family. The case of one 43 year-old single cocaine addict whose function declined markedly over a three year period illustrates this point. The patient had been a successful lawyer in independent practice until several years before when he reluctantly joined his family's business, in order to bolster it at a time of instability. He began using cocaine, in part because of his misgivings over relinquishing his professional career. He soon became addicted, and began to flounder at work and in his personal relations. His family became increasingly concerned as he began to spend most of his time at home in an intoxicated state, and they eventually sought out professional help in the hope of gaining some advice as to a proper course of action. Because the patient was financially dependent on the family it was possible to present him with the option of loss of support in the way of cancelled credit cards or charge accounts at local retail establishments should he not be willing to participate in some discussions regarding his drug problem.

Often such patients can be confronted in a concerned way in a situation in which they have no alternative but to comply with a therapeutic regimen. In this case, the patient agreed to go along with a plan for abstinence. An agreement was developed with the family which included his commitment to abstinence, paired with their continuing economic support. Subsequent individual sessions with him dealt with his considerable feelings of depression because of his social isolation and recent failures in business.

It was also agreed that he would undergo observed urine tests for cocaine, performed on a regular basis at a nearby laboratory, so as to assure both his family and me that he was not involved in further drug use. In matter of fact, these tests initially revealed continuing use of cocaine, but when confronted with the findings in a firm but supportive way, the patient eventually relinquished his drug use. The patient came to view the therapeutic endeavor positively, and after achieving abstinence for a protracted time, continued with psychotherapy primarily to address his conflicts over his career and his adaptation to a drug-free social life.

Adapting Individual Therapy to the Network Treatment

As noted above, network sessions are scheduled on a weekly basis at the outset of treatment. This is likely to compromise the number of individual contacts. Indeed, if sessions are held once a week, the patient may not be seen individually for a period of time. This may be perceived as a deprivation by the patient unless the individual therapy is presented as an opportunity for further growth *predicated* on achieving stable abstinence assured through work with the network.

When the individual therapy does begin, the traditional objectives of therapy must be ordered so as to accommodate the goals of the substance abuse treatment. For insight-oriented therapy, clarification of unconscious motivations is a primary objective; for supportive therapy, the bolstering of established constructive defenses is primary. In the therapeutic context which we are describing, however, the following objectives are given precedence.

Of first importance is the need to address exposure to substances of abuse, or exposure to cues which might precipitate cocaine use. Both patient and therapist should be sensitive to this matter and explore these situations as they arise. Secondly, a stable social context in an appropriate social environment—one conducive to abstinence with minimal disruption of life circumstances—should be supported. Considerations of minor disruptions in place of residence, friends, or job, need not be a primary issue for the patient with character disorder or neurosis, but they cannot go untended here. For a considerable period of time, the substance abuser is highly vulnerable to exacerbations of the addictive illness and must be viewed with the considerable caution, in some respects, as one treats the recently compensated psychotic.

Finally, after attending to these priorities, psychological conflicts which the patient must resolve, relative to his own growth, are considered. As the therapy continues, these come to assume a more prominent role. In the earlier phases, they are likely to directly reflect issues associated with previous drug use. Later, however, the tenor of treatment will come increasingly to resemble the traditional psychotherapeutic context. At this point the therapist is in the admirable position of working with a patient who, while exercising insight into his problems, is also motivated by the realization of a new and previously untapped potential.

REFERENCES

1. Stanton MD, Todd TC, and Associates. The family therapy of drug abuse and addiction. New York: *Guilford Press*, 1982.

2. Gallant DM, Rich A, Bey E, Terranova L. Group psychotherapy with married couples: a successful technique in New Orleans Alcoholism Clinic patients. *J La St Med Soc 1970*; 122:41–44.

3. Galanter M. Sociobiology and informal social controls of drinking. *J Studies Alcohol 1981*; 42:64–79.

4. Hayman M. Current attitudes to alcoholism of psychiatrists in Southern California. *Am J Psychiatry 1956*; 112:484–493.

5. Gawin FH, Kleber HD. Cocaine abuse treatment. *Arch Gen Psychiatry 1984*; 41:903–909.

6. Bale RN, Zarcone VP, Van Stone WW, et al. Three therapeutic communities. *Arch Gen Psychiatry 1984*; 41:185–191.

7. Galanter M. Use of the social and family network in individual therapy. In: Zimberg S, ed. Practical approaches to alcoholism psychotherapy. New York: *Plenum Publishing Corporation*, 1985:173–186.

8. Galanter M. Psychotherapy for alcohol and drug abuse: an approach based on learning theory. *J Psychiat Treatment and Evaluation 1983*; 5:551–556.

9. Steinglass P. Experimenting with family treatment approaches to alcoholism 1950–1975: a review. *Family Process 1976*; 15:97–123.

SELECTIVE GUIDE TO CURRENT REFERENCE SOURCES ON TOPICS DISCUSSED IN THIS ISSUE

Cocaine: Pharmacology, Addiction, and Therapy

James E. Raper, Jr., MSLS

Each issue of *Advances in Alcohol and Substance Abuse* features a section offering suggestions on where to look for further information on topics discussed in that issue. In this issue, our intent is to guide readers to selected sources of current information on cocaine abuse, addiction, and therapy.

Some reference sources utilize designated terminology (controlled vocabularies) which must be used to find material on topics of interest. For these a sample of available search terms has been indicated so that the reader can access suitable sources for his/her purposes. Other reference tools use keywords or free-text terms (generally from the title of the document or the name of the responsible agency or conference). In searching the latter, the user should also look under synonyms for the concept in question.

An asterisk (*) appearing before a published source indicates that

The author is affiliated with the Gustave L. and Janet W. Levy Library, The Mount Sinai Medical Center, Inc., One Gustave L. Levy Place, New York, NY 10029.

177

all or part of that source is in machine-readable form and can be accessed through an online database search. Database searching is recommended for retrieving sources of information that coordinates multiple concepts or subject areas. Most health sciences libraries offer database services, and many databases are now available for searching in ones office or home via microcomputer technology and subscriptions with database vendors.

Readers are encouraged to consult their librarians for further assistance before undertaking research on a topic.

Suggestions regarding the content and organization of this section are welcome.

INDEXING AND ABSTRACTING SOURCES

Place of publication, publisher, start date, and frequency of publication are noted.

Biological Abstracts (1926–) and *Biological Abstracts/RRM* (v.18, 1980–). Philadelphia, BioSciences Information Service, semimonthly.

> See: Abstracts and concept headings in behavioral biology, immunology, pharmacology, psychiatry, public health, and toxicology sections.
> See: Keyword-in-context subject index.

Chemical Abstracts. Columbus, Ohio, American Chemical Society, 1907– , weekly.

> See: *Index Guide* for cross-referencing and indexing policies.
> See: *General Subject Index* terms, such as drug dependence, drug-drug interactions, drug tolerance.
> See: Keyword subject indexes.

Criminal Justice Periodical Index. Ann Arbor, MI, Indexing Services, University Microfilms, 1975– , 3 times per year.

> See: Subject descriptors, such as cocaine, narcotic addicts.

Dissertation Abstracts International. Section A. Humanities and Social Sciences. Ann Arbor, MI, University Microfilms, v.30, 1969/70– , monthly.

> See: Keyword-in-context subject index.

Dissertation Abstracts International. Section B. The Sciences and Engineering. Ann Arbor, MI, University Microfilms, v.30, 1969/70– , monthly.

See: Keyword-in-context subject index.
Excerpta Medica: Clinical Biochemistry. Section 29. Amsterdam,
  The Netherlands, Excerpta Medica, v.27, 1973– , 32 issues per
  year.
  See: Subject index.
Excerpta Medica: Drug Dependence. Section 40. Amsterdam, The
  Netherlands, Excerpta Medica, v.8, 1980– , 6 issues per year.
  See: Subject index.
Excerpta Medica: Health Economics and Hospital Management.
  Section 36. Amsterdam, The Netherlands, Excerpta Medica, v.3,
  1973– , 8 issues per year.
  See: Subject index.
Excerpta Medica: Internal Medicine. Section 6. Amsterdam, The
  Netherlands, Excerpta Medica, 1947– , 30 issues per year.
  See: Subject index.
Excerpta Medica: Pharmacology. Section 30. Amsterdam, The
  Netherlands, Excerpta Medica, v.57, 1983– , 20 issues per year.
  See: Drug addiction section.
  See: Subject index.
Excerpta Medica: Psychiatry. Section 32. Amsterdam, The Neth-
  erlands, Excerpta Medica, v.22, 1969– , 20 issues per year.
  See: Addiction section.
  See: Subject index.
Excerpta Medica: Public Health, Social Medicine and Hygiene.
  Section 17. Amsterdam, The Netherlands, Excerpta Medica.
  1955– , 20 issues per year.
  See: Addiction, drug control sections.
  See: Subject index.
Excerpta Medica: Toxicology. Section 52. Amsterdam, The Neth-
  erlands, Excerpta Medica, 1983– , 20 issues per year.
  See: Subject index.
Index Medicus. (including *Bibliography of Medical Reviews*).
  Bethesda, MD, National Library of Medicine, 1960– , monthly.
  See: *MeSH* terms, such as cocaine, drug interactions, metha-
    done, substance abuse, substance dependence, substance
    use disorders.
Index to Scientific Reviews. Philadelphia, Institute for Scientific
  Information, 1974– , semiannual.
  See: Permuterm keyword subject index.
  See: Citation index.

International Pharmaceutical Abstracts. Washington, DC, American Society of Hospital Pharmacists, 1964– , semimonthly.
See: IPA subject terms, such as cocaine, dependence, drug abuse, rehabilitation facilities, toxicity.
Psychological Abstracts. Washington, DC, American Psychological Association, 1927– , monthly.
See: Index terms, such as addiction, cocaine, drug abuse, drug addiction, drug dependency, drug rehabilitation, drug usage.
Public Affairs Information Service Bulletin. New York, Public Affairs Information Service, v.55, 1969– , semimonthly.
See: PAIS subject headings, such as cocaine, drug abuse, drug addicts, methadone.
Science Citation Index. Philadelphia, Institute for Scientific Information, 1961– , bimonthly.
See: Permuterm keyword subject index.
See: Citation index.
Social Sciences Citation Index. Philadelphia, Institute for Scientific Information, 1966/70– , 3 issues per year.
See: Permuterm keyword subject index.
See: Citation index.
Social Work Research and Abstracts. New York, National Association of Social Workers, v.13, 1977– , quarterly.
See: Fields of service sections, such as alcoholism and drug addiction.
See: Subject index.
Sociological Abstracts. San Diego, CA, International Sociological Association, 1952/53– , 5 issues per year.
See: Subject index terms such as addict/addicts/addicted/ addictive/addiction, drug/drugs, drug addict/drug addicts/ drug addiction, methadone.

2. CURRENT AWARENESS PUBLICATIONS

Current Contents: Clinical Practice. Philadelphia, Institute for Scientific Information, 1973– , weekly.
See: Keyword index.
Current Contents: Life Sciences. Philadelphia, Institute for Scientific Information, v.10, 1967– , weekly.
See: Keyword index.

Current Contents: Social and Behavioral Sciences. Philadelphia, Institute for Scientific Information, v.6, 1974– , weekly. See: Keyword index.

3. BOOKS

Andrews, Theodora. *A Bibliography of Drug Abuse, Including Alcohol and Tobacco.* Littleton, CO, Libraries Unlimited, 1977– .

*Medical and Health Care Books and Serials in Print: An Index to Literature in the Health Sciences. New York, R.R. Bowker Co., annual.

    See: Library of Congress subject headings, such as cocaine, drug abuse, methadone hydrochloride, rehabilitation, rehabilitation centers.

*National Library of Medicine Current Catalog. Bethesda, MD, National Library of Medicine, 1966– , quarterly.

    See: *MeSH* terms as noted in Section 1 under *Index Medicus.*

O'Brien, Robert and Sidney Cohen. *The Encyclopedia of Drug Abuse.* New York, Facts on File Pub., 1984.

4. U.S. GOVERNMENT PUBLICATIONS

*Monthly Catalog of United States Government Publications. Washington, DC, U.S. Government, Printing Office, 1895– , monthly.

    See: Following agencies: Alcohol, Drug Abuse and Mental Health Administration, National Institute of Mental Health, National Institute on Drug Abuse.

    See: Subject headings, derived chiefly from the Library of Congress, such as cocaine, drug abuse, drug dependence, methadone maintenance, narcotic addicts, psychopharmacology.

    See: Keyword title index.

5. ONLINE BIBLIOGRAPHIC DATABASES

Only those databases which have no single print equivalents are included in this section. Print sources which have online database equivalents are noted throughout this guide by the asterisk (*) which appears before the title. If you do not have direct access to these databases consult your librarian for assistance.

DRUG INFO/ALCOHOL USE/ABUSE (Hazelden Foundation, Center City, MN, and Drug Information Service Center, College of Pharmacy, University of Minnesota, Minneapolis, MN.
   Use: Subject headings, such as addiction, cocaine, drug abuse, drug dependence, drug therapy, drug use, drug use pattern, methadone, rehabilitation.
   Use: Keywords.
LEGAL RESOURCE INDEX (Information Access Co., Belmont, CA.
   Use: Keywords.
MAGAZINE INDEX (Information Access Co., Belmont, CA).
   Use: Keywords.
MEDICAL AND PSYCHOLOGICAL PREVIEWS: MPPS (BRS Bibliographic Retrieval Services, Inc., Latham, NY; formerly *PRE-MED* and *PRE-PSYCH*).
   Use: Keywords.
MENTAL HEALTH ABSTRACTS (IFI/Plenum Data Co., Alexandria, VA.).
   Use: Keywords.
NATIONAL NEWSPAPER INDEX (Information Access Co., Belmont, CA).
   Use: Keywords.
NTIS (National Technical Information Service, U.S. Dept. of Commerce, Springfield, VA).
   Use: Keywords.
PSYCALERT (American Psychological Association, Washington, DC)
   Use: Keywords.

6. HANDBOOKS, DIRECTORIES, GRANT SOURCES, ETC.

Annual Register of Grant Support. Chicago, Marquis Academic Media/Marquis Who's Who, annual.
   See: Medicine, mental health, pharmacology, psychiatry, psychology sections.
Encyclopedia of Associations. Detroit, Gale Research Co., annual (occasional supplements between editions).

See: Subject index.
Foundation Directory. New York, The Foundation Center, biennial (updated between editions by *Foundation Directory Supplement*).
See: Index of foundations.
See: Index of foundations by state and city.
See: Index of donors, trustees, and administrators.
See: Index of fields of interest.
Research Awards Index. Bethesda, MD, National Institutes of Health, Division of Research Grants, annual.
See: Drug abuse terms in the index volume.

7. JOURNAL LISTINGS

Ulrich's International Periodicals Directory. New York, R. R. Bowker Co., annual (updated between editions by *Ulrich's Quarterly*).
See: Subject categories, such as drug abuse and alcoholism, medical sciences.

8. AUDIOVISUAL PROGRAMS

The Health Sciences Videolog. New York, Video Forum, 1981.
See: Subject index terms, such as drug abuse, drug dependence, drug interactions, narcotics.
National Library of Medicine Audiovisuals Catalog. Bethesda, MD, National Library of Medicine, 1977– , quarterly.
See: *MeSH* terms as noted in Section 1 under *Index Medicus*.

9. GUIDES TO UPCOMING MEETINGS

Scientific Meetings. San Diego, CA, Scientific Meetings Publications, quarterly.
See: Subject indexes.
See: Association listing.
World Meetings: Medicine. New York, Macmillan Pub. Co., quarterly.
See: Keyword index.
See: Sponsor directory and index.
World Meetings: Outside United States and Canada. New York, Macmillan Pub. Co., quarterly.

See: Keyword index.
See: Sponsor directory and index.
*World Meetings: Social & Behavioral Sciences, Human Services, &
Management.* New York, Macmillan Pub. Co., quarterly.
See: Subject index.
See: Sponsor directory and index.
World Meetings: United States and Canada. New York, Macmillan
Pub. Co., quarterly.
See: Keyword index.
See: Sponsor directory and index.

10. PROCEEDINGS OF MEETINGS

*Conference Papers Index. Louisville, KY, Data Courier, v.6,
1978– , monthly.
*Directory of Published Proceedings. Series SEMT. Science/
Engineering/Medicine/Technology.* White Plains, NY, InterDok
Corp., v.3, 1967– , monthly, except July–August, with annual
cumulations.
*Index to Scientific and Technical Proceedings. Philadelphia,
Institute for Scientific Information, 1978– , monthly with semi-
annual cumulations.

11. SPECIALIZED RESEARCH CENTERS

Research Centers Directory. 10th ed. Detroit, Gale Research Co.,
1986, c1985 (updated by *New Research Centers*).

12. SPECIAL LIBRARY COLLECTIONS

Ash, L., comp. *Subject Collections.* 6th ed. New York, R.R.
Bowker Co., 1985.
Directory of Special Libraries and Information Centers. 9th ed.
Detroit, Gale Research Co., 1985 (updated by *New Special
Libraries*).